Hudson
Taylor

J. Hudson Taylor

BETHANY HOUSE PUBLISHERS
MINNEAPOLIS, MINNESOTA 55438

Hudson Taylor
J. Hudson Taylor

This edition published by Bethany House Publishers by
arrangement with the China Inland Mission. Originally issued
under the title *A Retrospect*; also under the title
To China With Love.

Cover illustration by Brett Longley

Library of Congress Catalog Number 86-72977

ISBN   978-0-87123-951-8

Published by Bethany House Publishers
11400 Hampshire Avenue South
Bloomington, Minnesota 55438

Bethany House Publishers is a division of
Baker Publishing Group, Grand Rapids, Michigan.

Printed in the United States of America

Contents

THIS MAP SHOWS SOME OF THE CITIES VISITED BY HUDSON
TAYLOR IN HIS JOURNEYS FROM SHANGHAI

Foreword to the Seventeenth Edition

Hudson Taylor's life closed with the dawn of the present century, yet this his only autobiographical writing retains its charm and power. It tells the story of his youth and early experiences as a missionary in China, ending when the establishment of the China Inland Mission in 1865 brought him to the threshold of his real lifework. His place in the annals of the Christian church is assured on account of all he subsequently did and suffered to make the Gospel accessible to many millions of people living in inland China. Few men have been the instrument in God's hands for proclaiming the good news of His salvation to such a vast population and bringing so many Christian churches into being. An achievement of this magnitude prompts the inquiry: What kind of man was this? Many books have been written about him by others, but here in its simplest form is the essence of his spirit and character. It is not difficult to perceive that he was a man of prayer, faith, and likeness to Christ beyond the normal and therein lies the disturbing challenge of these pages. The Christian church has no profounder need than further demonstrations of such discipleship.

—David Bentley-Taylor

"Thou shalt remember all the way which
the Lord thy God led thee."

CHAPTER ONE

The Power of Prayer

THE FOLLOWING ACCOUNT of some of the experiences which eventually led to the formation of the China Inland Mission, and to its taking the form in which it has been developed, first appeared in the pages of *China's Millions*.[1] Many of those who read it there asked that it might appear in separate form. Miss Guinness incorporated it in the *Story of the China Inland Mission*, a record which contained the account of God's goodness to the beginning of 1894.[2] But because friends still ask for it in pamphlet form, for wider distribution, this edition is brought out.

Much of the material was taken from notes of addresses given in China during a conference of our missionaries; this will account for the direct and narrative form of the papers, which it has not been thought necessary to change.

It is always helpful to us to fix our attention

[1] The monthly magazine of the China Inland Mission has been published with this title since 1875.
[2] This book by Miss Guinness, subsequently Mrs. Howard Taylor, has long been superseded by other publications.

7

on the Godward aspect of Christian work; to
realize that the work of God does not mean so
much man's work for God, as God's own work
through man. Furthermore, in our privileged
position of fellow workers with Him, while fully
recognizing all the benefits and blessings to be
bestowed on a sin-stricken world through the
proclamation of the Gospel and spread of the
truth, we should never lose sight of the higher
aspect of our work—that of obedience to God,
of bringing glory to His name, of gladdening the
heart of our God and Father by living and serving as His beloved children.

Many circumstances connected with my own
early life and service presented this aspect of work
vividly to me; and as I think of some of them, I
am reminded of how much the cause of missions
is indebted to many who are never themselves
permitted to see the mission field—many, it may
be, who are unable to give largely of their sub-
stance, and who will be not a little surprised in
the Great Day to see how much the work has
been advanced by their love, their sympathy, and
their prayers.

For myself, and for the work that I have been
permitted to do for God, I owe an unspeakable
debt of gratitude to my beloved and honored
parents, who have passed away and entered into
rest, but the influence of whose lives will never
pass away.

Many years ago, probably about 1830, the
heart of my dear father, then himself an earnest
and successful evangelist at home, was deeply
stirred as to the spiritual state of China by read-

ing several books, and especially an account of
the travels of Captain Basil Hall. His circumstances were such as to preclude the hope of his
ever going to China for personal service, but he
was led to pray that if God should give him a
son, he might be called and privileged to labor
in the vast needy empire which was then apparently so sealed against the truth. I was not
aware of this desire or prayer myself until my
return to England, more than seven years after
I had sailed for China; but it was very interesting
then to know how prayer offered before my
birth had been answered in this matter.

All thought of my becoming a missionary was
abandoned for many years by my dear parents
on account of the feebleness of my health. When
the time came, however, God gave increased
health, and my life has been spared, and strength
has been given for not a little toilsome service
both in the mission field and at home, while
many stronger men and women have succumbed.

I had many opportunities in early years of
learning the value of prayer and of the Word of
God; for it was the delight of my dear parents to
point out that if there were any such Being as
God, to trust Him, to obey Him, and to be fully
given up to His service must of necessity be the
best and wisest course both for myself and others.
But in spite of these helpful examples and precepts my heart was unchanged. Often I had
tried to make myself a Christian; and failing of
course in such efforts, I began at last to think
that for some reason or other I could not be
saved, and that the best I could do was to take

my fill of this world, as there was no hope for
me beyond the grave.

While in this state of mind I came in contact
with persons holding skeptical and infidel views,
and accepted their teaching, only too thankful
for some hope of escape from the doom which,
if my parents were right and the Bible true,
awaited the impenitent. It may seem strange to
say it, but I have often felt thankful for the experience of this time of skepticism. The incon-
sistencies of Christian people, who, while professing to believe their Bibles, were yet content
to live just as they would if there were no such
Book, had been one of the strongest arguments
of my skeptical companions; and I frequently
felt at that time, and said that if I pretended to
believe the Bible I would at any rate attempt to
live by it, putting it fairly to the test, and if it
failed to prove true and reliable, I would throw
it overboard altogether. These views I retained
when the Lord was pleased to bring me to Himself; and I think I may say that since then I have
put God's Word to the test. Certainly it has
never failed me. I have never had reason to regret
the confidence I have placed in its promises, or
to deplore following the guidance I have found in
its directions.

Let me tell you how God answered the prayers
of my dear mother and my beloved sister, now
Mrs. Broomhall, for my conversion. On a day
which I shall never forget, when I was about
fifteen years of age, because my dear mother was
absent from home, I had a holiday, and in the
afternoon looked through my father's library to

find some book with which to while away the unoccupied hours. Nothing attracting me, I turned over a little basket of pamphlets, and selected from among them a Gospel tract which looked interesting, saying to myself, "There will be a story at the beginning, and a sermon or moral at the close: I will take the former and leave the latter for those who like it."

I sat down to read the little book in an utterly unconcerned state of mind, believing indeed at the time that if there were any salvation it was not for me, and with a distinct intention to put away the tract as soon as it should seem prosy. I may say that it was not uncommon in those days to call conversion "becoming serious"; and judging by the faces of some of its professors, it appeared to be a very serious matter indeed. Would it not be well if the people of God had always telltale faces, evincing the blessings and gladness of salvation so clearly that unconverted people might have to call conversion "becoming joyful" instead of "becoming serious"?

Little did I know at the time what was going on in the heart of my dear mother, seventy or eighty miles away. She rose from the dinner table that afternoon with an intense yearning for the conversion of her boy, and feeling that—absent from home, and having more leisure than she could otherwise secure—a special opportunity was afforded her of pleading with God on my behalf. She went to her room and turned the key in the door, resolved not to leave that spot until her prayers were answered. Hour after hour did that dear mother plead for me, until at length she could pray no longer, but was constrained to praise God for that which His Spirit taught her had already been accomplished—the conversion of her only son.

I in the meantime had been led in the way I have mentioned to take up this little tract, and while reading it was struck with the sentence, "The finished work of Christ." The thought passed through my mind, "Why does the author use this expression? Why not say the atoning or propitiatory work of Christ?" Immediately the words "It is finished" suggested themselves to my mind. What was finished? And I at once replied, "A full and perfect atonement and satisfaction for sin: the debt was paid by the Substitute; Christ died for our sins, and not for ours only, but also for the sins of the whole world." Then came the thought, "If the whole work was finished and the whole debt paid, what is there left for me to do?" And with this dawned the joyful conviction, as light was flashed into my soul by the Holy Spirit, that there was nothing in the world to be done but to fall down on one's knees, and accepting this Saviour and His salvation, to praise Him forevermore. Thus while my dear mother was praising God on her knees in her chamber, I was praising Him in the old warehouse to which I had gone alone to read this little book at my leisure.

Several days elapsed ere I ventured to make my beloved sister the confidante of my joy, and then only after she had promised not to tell anyone of my soul secret. When our dear mother came home a fortnight later, I was the first to meet her at the door, and to tell her I had such glad news to give. I can almost feel that dear mother's arms around my neck, as she pressed me to her bosom and said, "I know, my boy; I have been rejoicing for a fortnight in the glad tidings you have to tell me." "Why," I asked in surprise, "has Amelia broken her promise? She said she would tell no one." My dear mother assured me that it was not from any human source that she had learned the tidings, and went on to tell the little incident mentioned above. You will agree with me that it would be strange indeed if I were not a believer in the power of prayer.

Nor was that all. Some little time after, I picked up a pocketbook exactly like one of my own, and thinking that it was mine, opened it. The lines that caught my eye were an entry in the little diary, which belonged to my sister, to the effect that she would give herself daily to prayer until God should answer in the conversion of her brother. Exactly one month later the Lord was pleased to turn me from darkness to light.

Brought up in such a circle and saved under such circumstances, it was perhaps natural that from the beginning of my Christian life I was led to feel that the promises were very real, and that prayer was a sober matter-of-fact transacting business with God, whether on one's own behalf or on behalf of those for whom one sought His blessing.

CHAPTER TWO

The Call to Service

THE FIRST JOYS of conversion passed away after a time, and were succeeded by a period of painful deadness of soul, with much conflict. But this also came to an end, leaving a deepened sense of personal weakness and dependence on the Lord as the only Keeper as well as Saviour of His people. How sweet to the soul, wearied and disappointed in its struggles with sin, is the calm repose of trust in the Shepherd of Israel!

Not many months after my conversion, having a leisure afternoon, I retired to my own chamber to spend it largely in communion with God. Well do I remember that occasion. How in the gladness of my heart I poured out my soul before God; and again and again confessing my grateful love to Him who had done everything for me —who had saved me when I had given up all hope and even desire for salvation—I besought Him to give me some work to do for Him, as an outlet for love and gratitude; some self-denying service, no matter what it might be, however trying or however trivial; something with which He would be pleased, and that I might do for Him who had done so much for me. Well do I

14

remember, as in unreserved consecration I put myself, my life, my friends, my all, upon the altar, the deep solemnity that came over my soul with the assurance that my offering was accepted. The presence of God became unutterably real and blessed; and though but a child under sixteen, I remember stretching myself on the ground, and lying there silent before Him with unspeakable awe and unspeakable joy.

For what service I was accepted I knew not; but a deep consciousness that I was no longer my own took possession of me, which has never since been effaced. It has been a very practical consciousness. Two or three years later propositions of an unusually favorable nature were made to me with regard to medical study, on the condition of my becoming apprenticed to the medical man who was my friend and teacher. But I felt I dared not accept any binding engagement such as was suggested. I was not my own to give myself away; for I knew not when or how He whose alone I was, and for whose disposal I felt I must ever keep myself free, might call for service.

Within a few months of this time of consecration the impression was wrought into my soul that it was in China the Lord wanted me. It seemed to me highly probable that the work to which I was thus called might cost my life; for China was not then open as it is now. But few missionary societies had at that time workers in China, and but few books on the subject of China missions were accessible to me. I learned, however, that the Congregational minister of my native town possessed a copy of Medhurst's *China*, and I called upon him to ask a loan of the book. This he kindly granted, asking me why I wished to read it. I told him that God had called me to spend my life in missionary service in that land. "And how do you propose to go there?" he inquired. I answered that I did not at all know; that it seemed to me probable that I should need to do as the Twelve and the Seventy had done in Judea—go without purse or scrip, relying on Him who had called me to supply all my need. Kindly placing his hand upon my shoulder, the minister replied, "Ah, my boy, as you grow older you will get wiser than that. Such an idea would do very well in the days when Christ Himself was on earth, but not now."

I have grown older since then, but not wiser. I am more than ever convinced that if we were to take the directions of our Master and the assurances He gave to His first disciples more fully as our guide, we should find them to be just as suited to our times as to those in which they were originally given.

Medhurst's book on China emphasized the value of medical missions there, and this directed my attention to medical studies as a valuable mode of preparation.

My beloved parents neither discouraged nor encouraged my desire to engage in missionary work. They advised me, with such convictions, to use all the means in my power to develop the resources of body, mind, heart, and soul, and to wait prayerfully upon God, quite willing, should He show me that I was mistaken, to follow His guidance, or to go forward if in due time He should open the way to missionary service. The importance of this advice I have often since had occasion to prove. I began to take more exercise in the open air to strengthen my physique. My featherbed I had taken away, and sought to dispense with as many other home comforts as I could, in order to prepare myself for rougher lines of life. I began also to do what Christian work was in my power, in the way of tract distribution, Sunday school teaching, and visiting the poor and sick, as opportunity afforded.

After a time of preparatory study at home, I went to Hull for medical and surgical training. There I became assistant to a doctor who was connected with the Hull school of medicine, and was surgeon also to a number of factories, which brought many accident cases to our dispensary, and gave me the opportunity of seeing and practicing the minor operations of surgery.

And here an event took place that I must not omit to mention. Before leaving home my attention was drawn to the subject of setting apart the first fruits of one's increase and a proportionate part of one's possessions to the Lord's service. I thought it well to study the question with my Bible in hand before I went away from home, and was placed in circumstances which might bias my conclusions by the pressure of surrounding wants and cares. I was thus led to the determination to set apart not less than one-tenth of whatever moneys I might earn or become possessed of for the Lord's service. The salary I received as medical assistant in Hull at the time now referred to would have allowed me with ease to do this. But owing to changes in the family of my kind friend and employer, it was necessary for me to reside out of doors. Comfortable quarters were secured with a relative, and in addition to the sum determined on as remuneration for my services I received the exact amount I had to pay for board and lodging.

Now arose in my mind the question, Ought not this sum also to be tithed? It was surely a part of my income, and I felt that if it had been a question of government income tax it certainly would not have been excluded. On the other hand, to take a tithe from the whole would not leave me sufficient for other purposes; and for some little time I was much embarrassed to know what to do. After much thought and prayer I was led to leave the comfortable quarters and happy circle in which I was now residing, and to engage a little lodging in the suburbs—a sitting room and bedroom in one—undertaking to board myself. In this way I was able without difficulty to tithe the whole of my income; and while I felt the change a good deal, it was attended with no small blessing.

More time was given in my solitude to the study of the Word of God, to visiting the poor, and to evangelistic work on summer evenings than would otherwise have been the case. Brought into contact in this way with many who were in distress, I soon saw the privilege of still further economizing, and found it not difficult to give away much more than the proportion of my income I had at first intended.

About this time a friend drew my attention to the question of the personal and premillennial coming of our Lord Jesus Christ, and gave me a list of passages bearing upon it, without note or comment, advising me to ponder the subject. For a while I gave much time to studying the Scriptures about it, with the result that I was led to see that this same Jesus who left our earth in His resurrection body was so to come again, that His feet were to stand on the Mount of Olives, and that He was to take possession of the temporal throne of His father David which was promised before His birth. I saw, further, that all through the New Testament the coming of the Lord was the great hope of His people, and was always appealed to as the strongest motive for consecration and service, and as the greatest comfort in trial and affliction. I learned too that the period of His return for His people was not revealed, and that it was their privilege, from day to day and from hour to hour, to live as men who wait for the Lord; that thus living it was immaterial, so to speak, whether He should or should not come at any particular hour, the important thing being to be so ready for Him as to be able, whenever He might appear, to give an account of one's stewardship with joy, and not with grief.

The effect of this blessed hope was a thoroughly practical one. It led me to look carefully through my little library to see if there were any books there that were not needed or likely to be of further service, and to examine my small wardrobe, to be quite sure that it contained nothing that I should be sorry to give an account of should the Master come at once. The result was that the library was considerably diminished, to the benefit of some poor neighbors, and to the far greater benefit of my own soul, and that I found I had articles of clothing also which might be put to better advantage in other directions.

It has been very helpful to me from time to time through life, as occasion has served, to act again in a similar way; and I have never gone through my house, from basement to attic, with this object in view, without receiving a great accession of spiritual joy and blessing. I believe we are all in danger of accumulating—it may be from thoughtlessness, or from pressure of occupation—things which would be useful to others, while not needed by ourselves, and the retention of which entails loss of blessing. If the whole resources of the Church of God were well utilized, how much more might be accomplished! How many poor might be fed, and naked clothed, and to how many of those as yet unreached the Gospel might be carried! Let me advise this line of things as a constant habit of mind, and a profitable course to be practically adopted whenever circumstances permit.

CHAPTER THREE

Preparation for Service

HAVING NOW THE TWOFOLD OBJECT in view of accustoming myself to endure hardness, and of economizing in order to be able more largly to assist those among whom I spent a good deal of time laboring in the Gospel, I soon found that I could live upon very much less than I had previously thought possible. Butter, milk, and other such luxuries I soon ceased to use; and I found that by living mainly on oatmeal and rice, with occasional variations, a very small sum was sufficient for my needs. In this way I had more than two-thirds of my income available for other purposes; and my experience was that the less I spent on myself and the more I gave away, the fuller of happiness and blessing did my soul become. Unspeakable joy all the day long, and every day, was my happy experience. God, even my God, was a living, bright reality; and all I had to do was joyful service.

It was to me a very grave matter, however, to contemplate going out to China, far away from all human aid, there to depend upon the living God alone for protection, supplies, and help of every kind. I felt that one's spiritual muscles required strengthening for such an undertaking. There was no doubt that if faith did not fail, God would not fail; but, then, what if one's faith should prove insufficient? I had not at that time learned that even "if we believe not, he abideth faithful, he cannot deny himself"; and it was consequently a very serious question to my mind, not whether *He* was faithful, but whether I had strong enough faith to warrant my embarking in the enterprise set before me.

I thought to myself, "When I get out to China, I shall have no claim on anyone for anything; my only claim will be on God. How important, therefore, to learn before leaving England to move man, through God, by prayer alone!"

At Hull my kind employer, always busily occupied, wished me to remind him whenever my salary became due. This I determined not to do directly, but to ask that God would bring the fact to his recollection, and thus encourage me by answering prayer. At one time, as the day drew near for the payment of a quarter's salary, I was as usual much in prayer about it. The time arrived, but my kind friend made no allusion to the matter. I continued praying, and days passed on, but he did not remember, until at length, on settling up my weekly accounts one Saturday night, I found myself possessed of only a single coin—one half-crown piece. Still I had hitherto had no lack, and I continued in prayer.

That Sunday was a very happy one. As usual my heart was full and brimming over with blessing. After attending divine service in the morning, my afternoons and evenings were filled with

Gospel work in the various lodginghouses I was accustomed to visit in the lowest part of the town. At such times it almost seemed to me as if Heaven were begun below, and that all that could be looked for was an enlargement of one's capacity for joy, not a truer filling than I possessed. After concluding my last service about ten o'clock that night, a poor man asked me to go and pray with his wife, saying that she was dying. I readily agreed, and on the way to his house asked him why he had not sent for the priest, as his accent told me he was an Irishman. He had done so, he said, but the priest refused to come without a payment of eighteenpence, which the man did not possess, as the family was starving. Immediately it occurred to my mind that all the money I had in the world was the solitary half crown, and that it was in one coin; moreover, that while the basin of water gruel I usually took for supper was awaiting me, and there was sufficient in the house for breakfast in the morning, I certainly had nothing for dinner on the coming day.

Somehow or other there was at once a stoppage in the flow of joy in my heart; but instead of reproving myself I began to reprove the poor man, telling him that it was very wrong to have allowed matters to get into such a state as he described, and that he ought to have applied to the relieving officer. His answer was that he had done so, and was told to come at eleven o'clock the next morning, but he feared that his wife might not live through the night. "Ah," thought I, "if only I had two shillings and a sixpence instead of this half crown, how gladly would I give these poor people one shilling of it!" But to part with the half crown was far from my thoughts. I little dreamed that the real truth of the matter simply was that I could trust in God plus one-and-sixpence, but was not yet prepared to trust Him only, without any money at all in my pocket.

My conductor led me into a court, down which I followed with some degree of nervousness. I had found myself there before, and at my last visit had been very roughly handled, while my tracts were torn to pieces, and I received such a warning not to come again that I felt more than a little concerned. Still, it was the path of duty, and I followed on. Up a miserable flight of stairs, into a wretched room, he led me; and oh, what a sight there presented itself to our eyes! Four or five poor children stood about, their sunken cheeks and temples all telling unmistakably the story of slow starvation; and lying on a wretched pallet was a poor exhausted mother, with a tiny infant thirty-six hours old, moaning rather than crying at her side, for it too seemed spent and failing. "Ah!" thought I, "if I had two shillings and a sixpence instead of half a crown, how gladly should they have one-and-sixpence of it!" But still a wretched unbelief prevented me from obeying the impulse to relieve their distress at the cost of all I possessed.

It will scarcely seem strange that I was unable to say much to comfort these poor people. I needed comfort myself. I began to tell them, however, that they must not be cast down, that though their circumstances were very distressing, there was a kind and loving Father in Heaven; but something within me said, "You hypocrite, telling these unconverted people about a kind and loving Father in Heaven, and not prepared yourself to trust Him without half a crown!" I was nearly choked. How gladly would I have compromised with conscience if I had had a florin and a sixpence! I would have given the florin thankfully and kept the rest; but I was not yet prepared to trust in God alone, without the sixpence.

To talk was impossible under these circumstances; yet, strange to say, I thought I should have no difficulty in praying. Prayer was a delightful occupation to me in those days; time thus spent never seemed wearisome, and I knew nothing of lack of words. I seemed to think that all I should have to do would be to kneel down and engage in prayer, and that relief would come to them and to myself together. "You asked me to come and pray with your wife," I said to the man, "let us pray." And I knelt down. But scarcely had I opened my lips with "Our Father who art in heaven" than conscience said within, "Dare you mock God? Dare you kneel down and call Him Father with that half crown in your pocket?" Such a time of conflict came upon me then as I have never experienced before or since. How I got through that form of prayer I know not, and whether the words uttered were connected or disconnected I cannot tell; but I arose from my knees in great distress of mind.

The poor father turned to me and said, "You

see what a terrible state we are in, sir; if you can help us, for God's sake, do!" Just then the word flashed into my mind, "Give to him that asketh of thee," and in the word of a King there is power. I put my hand into my pocket, and slowly drawing forth the half crown, gave it to the man, telling him that it might seem a small matter for me to relieve them, seeing that I was comparatively well off, but that in parting with that coin I was giving him my all; what I had been trying to tell him was indeed true—God really was a Father, and might be trusted. The joy all came back in full flood tide to my heart; I could say anything and feel it then, and the hindrance to blessing was gone—gone, I trust, forever.

Not only was the poor woman's life saved, but I realized that my life was saved too! It might have been a wreck—would have been a wreck probably, as a Christian life—had not grace at that time conquered, and the striving of God's Spirit been obeyed. I well remember how that night, as I went home to my lodgings, my heart was as light as my pocket. The lonely, deserted streets resounded with a hymn of praise which I could not restrain. When I took my basin of gruel before retiring, I would not have exchanged it for a prince's feast. I reminded the Lord as I knelt at my bedside of His own Word, that he who giveth to the poor lendeth to the Lord: I asked Him not to let my loan be a long one, or I should have no dinner next day: and with peace within and peace without, I spent a happy, restful night.

Next morning for breakfast my plate of porridge remained, and before it was consumed the postman's knock was heard at the door. I was not in the habit of receiving letters on Monday, as my parents and most of my friends refrained from posting on Saturday; so that I was somewhat surprised when the landlady came in holding a letter or packet in her wet hand covered by her apron. I looked at the letter, but could not make out the handwriting. It was either a strange hand or a feigned one, and the postmark was blurred. Where it came from I could not tell. On opening the envelope I found nothing written within; but inside a sheet of blank paper was folded a pair of kid gloves, from which, as I opened them in astonishment, half a sovereign fell to the ground. "Praise the Lord!" I exclaimed; "400 per cent for twelve hours' investment; that is good interest. How glad the merchants of Hull would be if they could lend their money at such a rate!" I then and there determined that a bank which could not break should have my savings or earnings as the case might be —a determination I have not yet learned to regret.

I cannot tell you how often my mind has recurred to this incident, or all the help it has been to me in circumstances of difficulty in after-life. If we are faithful to God in little things, we shall gain experience and strength that will be helpful to us in the more serious trials of life.

CHAPTER FOUR

Further Answers to Prayer

THE REMARKABLE and gracious deliverance I have spoken of was a great joy to me, as well as a strong confirmation of faith; but of course ten shillings, however economically used, will not go very far, and it was nonetheless necessary to continue in prayer, asking that the larger supply which was still due might be remembered and paid. All my petitions, however, appeared to remain unanswered; and before a fortnight had elapsed I found myself pretty much in the same position that I had occupied on the Sunday night already made so memorable. Meanwhile, I continued pleading with God, more and more earnestly, that He would graciously remind my employer that my salary was overdue. Of course it was not the want of money that distressed me —that could have been had at any time for the asking—but the question uppermost in my mind was this: "Can I go to China? Or will my want of faith and power with God prove to be so serious an obstacle as to preclude my entering upon this much-prized service?"

As the week drew to a close I felt exceedingly embarrassed. There was not only myself to consider; on Saturday night a payment was due to my Christian landlady which I knew she could not well dispense with. Ought I not, for her sake, to speak about the matter of the salary? Yet to do so would be, to myself at any rate, the admission that I was not fitted to undertake a missionary enterprise. I gave nearly the whole of Thursday and Friday—all the time not occupied in my necessary employment—to the earnest wrestling with God in prayer. But still on Saturday morning I was in the same position as before. And now my earnest cry was for guidance as to whether it was my duty to break silence and speak to my employer, or whether I should continue to wait the Father's time. As far as I could judge, I received the assurance that to wait His time was best; and that God in some way or other would interpose on my behalf. So I waited, my heart being now at rest and the burden gone.

About five o'clock that Saturday afternoon, when the doctor had finished writing his prescriptions, his last circuit for the day being taken, he threw himself back in his armchair, as he was wont, and began to speak of the things of God. He was a truly Christian man, and many seasons of very happy spiritual fellowship we had together. I was busily watching, at the time, a pan in which a decoction was boiling that required a good deal of attention. It was indeed fortunate for me that it was so, for without any obvious connection with what had been going on, all at once he said, "By the bye, Taylor, is not your salary due again?" My emotion may be imagined! I had to swallow two or three times before I could answer. With my eye fixed on the pan and my back to the doctor, I told him as quietly as I could that it was overdue some little time. How thankful I felt at that moment! God surely had heard my prayer, and caused him in His time of my great need, to remember the salary without any word or suggestion from me. He replied, "Oh, I am so sorry you did not remind me! You know how busy I am; I wish I had thought of it a little sooner, for only this afternoon I sent all the money I had to the bank, otherwise I would pay you at once." It is impossible to describe the revulsion of feeling caused by this unexpected statement. I knew not what to do. Fortunately for me my pan boiled up, and I had a good reason for rushing with it from the room. Glad indeed I was to get away, and keep out of sight until after the doctor had returned to his house, and most thankful that he had not perceived my emotion.

As soon as he was gone I had to seek my little sanctum, and pour out my heart before the Lord for some time, before calmness—and more than calmness—thankfulness, and joy were restored to me. I felt that God had His own way, and was not going to fail me. I had sought to know His will early in the day, and as far as I could judge had received guidance to wait patiently; and now God was going to work for me in some other way.

That evening was spent, as my Saturday evenings usually were, in reading the Word and preparing the subjects on which I expected to speak in the various lodginghouses on the morrow. I waited, perhaps, a little longer than usual. At last, about ten o'clock, there being no interruption of any kind, I put on my overcoat, and was preparing to leave for home, rather thankful to know that by that time I should have to let myself in with the latch-key, as my landlady retired early to rest. There was certainly no help for that night; but perhaps God would interpose for me by Monday, and I might be able to pay my landlady early in the week the money I would have given her before, had it been possible.

Just as I was preparing to turn down the gas, I heard the doctor's step in the garden which lay between the dwelling house and surgery. He was laughing to himself very heartily, as though greatly amused by something. Entering the surgery, he asked for the ledger, and told me that, strange to say, one of his richest patients had just come to pay his doctor's bill—was it not an odd thing to do? It never struck me that it might have any bearing on my own particular case, or I might have felt embarrassed; but looking at it simply from the position of an uninterested spectator, I also was highly amused that a man who was rolling in wealth should come after ten o'clock at night to pay a doctor's bill, which he could any day have met by a check with the greatest ease. It appeared that somehow or other he could not rest with this on his mind and had been constrained to come at that unusual hour to discharge his liability.

The account was duly receipted in the ledger, and the doctor was about to leave, when suddenly he turned, and handing me some of the bank notes just received, said, to my surprise and thankfulness, "By the way, Taylor, you might as well take these notes; I have not any change, but can give you the balance next week." Again I was left—my feelings undiscovered—to go back to my own little closet and praise the Lord with a joyful heart that after all I might go to China.

To me the incident was not a trivial one; and to recall it sometimes, in circumstances of great difficulty, in China or elsewhere, has proved no small comfort and strength.

By and by the time drew near when it was thought desirable that I should leave Hull to attend the medical course of the London Hospital. A little while spent there, and then I had every reason to believe that my lifework in China would begin. But much as I had rejoiced at the willingness of God to hear and answer prayer and to help His half-trusting, half-timid child, I felt that I could not go to China without having still further developed and tested my power to rest upon His faithfulness, and a marked opportunity for doing so was providentially afforded me.

My dear father had offered to bear all the expense of my stay in London. I knew, however, that, owing to recent losses, it would mean a considerable sacrifice for him to undertake this just when it seemed necessary for me to go forward. I had recently become acquainted with the Committee of the Chinese Evangelization Society, in connection with which I ultimately left for China, and especially with its secretary, my esteemed and much-loved friend, Mr. George

Pearse, then of the Stock Exchange, but now and for many years himself a missionary. Not knowing of my father's proposition, the Committee also kindly offered to bear my expenses while in London. When these proposals were first made to me, I was not quite clear as to what I ought to do, and in writing to my father and the secretaries, told them that I would take a few days to pray about the matter before deciding any course of action. I mentioned to my father that I had had this offer from the society, and told the secretaries also of his proffered aid.

Subsequently, while waiting upon God in prayer for guidance, it became clear to my mind that I could without difficulty decline both offers. The secretaries of the society would not know that I had cast myself wholly on God for supplies, and my father would conclude that I had accepted the other offer. I therefore wrote declining both propositions, and felt that without any one having either care or anxiety on my account I was simply in the hands of God, and that He, who knew my heart, if He wished to encourage me to go to China, would bless my effort to depend upon Him alone at home.

CHAPTER FIVE

Life in London

I MUST NOT NOW ATTEMPT to detail the ways in which the Lord was pleased—often to my surprise, as well as to my delight—to help me from time to time. I soon found that it was not possible to live quite as economically in London as in Hull. To lessen expenses I shared a room with a cousin, four miles from the hospital, providing myself with board; and after various experiments I found that the most economical way was to live almost exclusively on brown bread and water. Thus I was able to make the means that God gave me last as long as possible. Some of my expenses I could not diminish, but my board was largely within my own control. A large twopenny loaf of brown bread, purchased daily on my long walk from the hospital, furnished me with supper and breakfast, and on that diet, with a few apples for lunch, I managed to walk eight or nine miles a day, besides being a good deal on foot while attending the practice of the hospital and the medical school.

One incident that occurred just about this time I must refer to. The husband of my former landlady in Hull was chief officer of a ship that sailed

from London, and by receiving his half-pay
monthly and remitting it to her I was able to
save her the cost of a commission. This I had
been doing for several months, when she wrote
requesting that I would obtain the next payment
as early as possible, as her rent was almost due,
and she depended upon that sum to meet it. The
request came at an inconvenient time. I was
working hard for an examination in the hope of
obtaining a scholarship which would be of service
to me, and felt that I could ill afford the time to
go during the busiest part of the day to the city
and procure the money. I had, however, sufficient
of my own in hand to enable me to send the
required sum. I made the remittance therefore
purposing as soon as the examination was over to
go and draw the regular allowance with which to
refund myself.

Before the time of examination the medical
school was closed for a day, on account of the
funeral of the Duke of Wellington, and I had an
opportunity of going at once to the office, which
was situated in a street off Cheapside, and apply-
ing for the due amount. To my surprise and dismay the clerk told me that he could not pay it, as
the officer in question had run away from his
ship and gone to the gold diggings.

"Well," I remarked, "that is very inconvenient
for me, as I have already advanced the money,
and I know his wife will have no means of re-
paying it." The clerk said he was sorry, but could
of course only act according to orders; so there
was no help for me in that direction. A little
more time and thought, however, brought the

comforting conclusion to my mind, that as I was depending on the Lord for everything, and His means were not limited, it was a small matter to be brought a little sooner or later into the position of needing fresh supplies from Him; and so the joy and the peace were not long interfered with.

Very soon after this, possibly the same evening, while sewing together some sheets of paper on which to take notes of the lectures, I accidentally pricked the first finger of my right hand, and in a few moments forgot all about it. The next day at the hospital I continued dissecting as before. The body was that of a person who had died of fever, and was more than usually disagreeable and dangerous. I need scarcely say that those of us who were at work upon it dissected with special care, knowing that the slightest scratch might cost us our lives. Before the morning was far advanced I began to feel very weary, and while going through the surgical wards at noon was obliged to run out, being suddenly very sick—a most unusual circumstance with me, as I took but little food and nothing that could disagree with me. After feeling faint for some time, a draught of cold water revived me, and I was able to rejoin the students. I became more and more unwell, however, and ere the afternoon lecture on surgery was over found it impossible to hold the pencil and continue taking notes. By the time the next lecture was through, my whole arm and right side were full of severe pain, and I was both looking and feeling very ill.

Finding that I could not resume work, I went

into the dissecting room to bind up the portion I was engaged upon and put away my apparatus, and said to the demonstrator, who was a very skilled surgeon, "I cannot think what has come over me," describing the symptoms. "Why," said he, "what has happened is clear enough: you must have cut yourself in dissecting, and you know that this is a case of malignant fever." I assured him that I had been most careful, and was quite certain that I had no cut or scratch. "Well," he replied, "you certainly must have had one"; and he very closely scrutinized my hand to find it, but in vain. All at once it occurred to me that I had pricked my finger the night before and I asked him if it were possible that a prick from a needle, at that time, could have been still unclosed. His opinion was that this was probably the cause of the trouble, and he advised me to get a hansom (cab), drive home as fast as I could, and arrange my affairs forthwith. "For," he said, "you are a dead man."

My first thought was one of sorrow that I could not go to China; but very soon came the feeling, "Unless I am greatly mistaken, I have work to do in China, and shall not die." I was glad, however, to take the opportunity of speaking to my medical friend, who was a confirmed skeptic as to things spiritual, of the joy that the prospect of perhaps soon being with my Master gave me; telling him at the same time that I did not think I should die, as, unless I were much mistaken, I had work to do in China; and if so, however severe the struggle, I must be brought through. "That is all very well," he answered, "but you get a hansom and drive home as fast as you can. You have no time to lose, for you will soon be incapable of winding up your affairs."

I smiled a little at the idea of my driving home in a hansom, for by this time my means were too exhausted to allow of such a proceeding, and I set out to walk the distance if possible. Before long, however, my strength gave way, and I felt it was no use to attempt to reach home by walking. Availing myself of an omnibus from Whitechapel Church to Farringdon Street, and another from Farringdon Street onwards, I reached, in great suffering, the neighborhood of Soho Square, behind which I lived. On going into the house I got some hot water from the servant, and charging her very earnestly—literally as a dying man— to accept eternal life as the gift of God through Jesus Christ, I bathed my head and lanced the finger, hoping to let out some of the poisoned blood. The pain was very severe; I fainted away, and was for some time unconscious, so long that when I came to myself I found that I had been carried to bed.

An uncle of mine who lived near at hand had come in, and sent for his own medical man, an assistant surgeon at the Westminster Hospital. I assured my uncle that medical help would be of no service to me, and that I did not wish to go to the expense involved. He, however, quieted me on this score, saying that he had sent for his own doctor, and that the bill would be charged to himself. When the surgeon came and learned all the particulars, he said, "Well, if you have been living moderately, you may pull through; but if you have been going in for beer and that sort of thing, there is no manner of chance for you." I thought that if sober living was to do anything, few could have a better chance, as little but bread and water had been my diet for a good while past. I told him I had lived abstemiously, and found that it helped me in study. "But now," he said, "you must keep up your strength, for it will be a pretty hard struggle." And he ordered me a bottle of port wine every day, and as many chops as I could consume. Again I smiled inwardly, having no means for the purchase of such luxuries. This difficulty, however, was met by my kind uncle, who sent me at once all that was needed.

I was much concerned, notwithstanding the agony I suffered, that my dear parents should not be made acquainted with my state. Thought and prayer had satisfied me that I was not going to die, but that there was indeed a work for me to do in China. If my dear parents should come up and find me in that condition, I must lose the opportunity of seeing how God was going to work for me, now that my money had almost come to an end. So, after prayer for guidance, I obtained a promise from my uncle and cousin not to write to my parents, but to leave me to communicate with them myself. I felt it was a very distinct answer to prayer when they gave me this promise, and I took care to defer all communication with them myself until the crisis was past and the worst of the attack over. At home they knew that I was working hard for an examination, and did not wonder at my silence.

Days and nights of suffering passed slowly by; but at length, after several weeks, I was sufficiently restored to leave my room; and then I learned that two men, though not from the London Hospital, who had had dissection wounds at the same time as myself, had both succumbed, while I was spared in answer to prayer to work for God in China.

CHAPTER SIX

Strengthened by Faith

ONE DAY THE DOCTOR coming in found me on the sofa, and was surprised to learn that with assistance I had walked downstairs. "Now," he said, "the best thing you can do is to get off to the country as soon as you feel equal to the journey. You must rusticate until you have recovered a fair amount of health and strength, for if you begin your work too soon the consequences may still be serious." When he had left, as I lay very exhausted on the sofa, I just told the Lord all about it, and that I was refraining from making my circumstances known to those who would delight to meet my need, in order that my faith might be strengthened by receiving help from Himself in answer to prayer alone. What was I to do? And I waited for His answer.

It seemed to me as if He were directing my mind to the conclusion to go again to the shipping office, and inquire about the wages I had been unable to draw. I reminded the Lord that I could not afford to take a conveyance, and that it did not seem at all likely that I should succeed in getting the money, and asked whether this impulse was not a mere clutching at a straw, some mental process of my own, rather than His guidance and teaching. After prayer, however, and renewed waiting upon God, I was confirmed in my belief that He Himself was teaching me to go to the office.

The next question was, "How am I to go?" I had had to seek help in coming downstairs, and the place was at least two miles away. The assurance was brought vividly home to me that whatever I asked of God in the name of Christ would be done, that the Father might be glorified in the Son; that what I had to do was to seek strength for the long walk, to receive it by faith, and to set out upon it. Unhesitatingly I told the Lord that I was quite willing to take the walk if He would give me the strength. I asked in the name of Christ that the strength might be immediately given; and sending the servant up to my room for my hat and stick, I set out, not to *attempt* to walk, but to *walk* to Cheapside.

Although undoubtedly strengthened by faith, I never took so much interest in shop windows as I did upon that journey. At every second or third step I was glad to lean a little against the plate glass, and take time to examine the contents of the windows before passing on. It needed a special effort of faith when I got to the bottom of Farringdon Street to attempt the toilsome ascent of Snow Hill: there was no Holborn Viaduct in those days, and it had to be done. God did wonderfully help me, and in due time I reached Cheapside, turned into the by-street in which the office was found, and sat down much exhausted on the steps leading to the first floor, which was my destination. I felt my position to be a little peculiar—sitting there on the steps, so evidently spent—and the gentlemen who rushed up and downstairs looked at me with an inquiring gaze. After a little rest, however, and a further season of prayer, I succeeded in climbing the staircase, and to my comfort found in the office the clerk with whom I had hitherto dealt in the matter. Seeing me looking pale and exhausted, he kindly inquired as to my health, and I told him that I had had a serious illness, and was ordered to the country, but thought it well to call first, and make further inquiry, lest there should have been any mistake about the mate having run off to the gold diggings. "Oh," he said, "I am so glad you have come, for it turns out that it was an able seaman of the same name that ran away. The mate is still on board; the ship has just reached Gravesend, and will be up very soon. I shall be glad to give you the half-pay up to date, for doubtless it will reach his wife more safely through you. We all know what temptations beset the men when they arrive at home after a voyage."

Before, however, giving me the sum of money, he insisted upon my coming inside and sharing his lunch. I felt it was the Lord indeed who was providing for me, and accepted his offer with thankfulness. When I was refreshed and rested, he gave me a sheet of paper to write a few lines to the wife, telling her of the circumstances. On my way back I procured in Cheapside a money order for the balance due to her, and posted it; and returning home again, felt myself now quite justified in taking an omnibus as far as it would serve me.

Very much better the next morning, after seeing to some little matters that I had to settle, I made my way to the surgery of the doctor who had attended me, feeling that, although my uncle was prepared to pay the bill, it was right for me, now that I had some money in hand, to ask for the account myself. The kind surgeon refused to allow me, as a medical student, to pay anything for his attendance; but he had supplied me with quinine, which he allowed me to pay for to the extent of eight shillings. When that was settled, I saw that the sum left was just sufficient to take me home; and to my mind the whole thing seemed a wonderful interposition of God on my behalf.

I knew that the surgeon was skeptical, and told him that I should very much like to speak to him freely, if I might do so without offense; that I felt that under God I owed my life to his kind care, and wished very earnestly that he himself might become a partaker of the same precious faith that I possessed. So I told him my reason for being in London, and about my circumstances, and why I had declined the help of both my father and the officers of the society in connection with which it was probable that I should go to China. I told him of the recent providential dealing of God with me, and how apparently hopeless my position had been the day before, when he had ordered me to go to the country, unless I would reveal my need, which I had determined not to do. I described to him the mental exercises I had gone through; but when I added that I had actually got up from the sofa and walked to Cheapside, he looked at me incredulously, and said, "Impossible! Why, I left you lying there more like a ghost than a man." And I had to assure him again and again that, strengthened by faith, the walk had really been taken. I told him also what money was left to me, and what payments there had been to make, and showed him that just sufficient remained to take me home to Yorkshire, providing for needful refreshment by the way and the omnibus journey at the end.

My kind friend was completely broken down, and said with tears in his eyes, "I would give all the world for a faith like yours." I, on the other hand, had the joy of telling him that it was to be obtained without money and without price. We never met again. When I came back to town, restored to health and strength, I found that he had had a stroke, and left for the country; and I subsequently learned that he never rallied. I was able to gain no information as to his state of mind when taken away; but I have always felt very thankful that I had the opportunity, and embraced it, of bearing the testimony for God. I cannot but entertain the hope that the Master Himself was speaking to him through His dealings with me, and that I shall meet him again in the Better Land. It would be no small joy to be welcomed by him, when my own service is over.

The next day found me in my dear parents' home. My joy in the Lord's help and deliverance was so great that I was unable to keep it to myself, and before my return to London my dear mother knew the secret of my life for some time past. I need scarcely say that when I went up again to town I was not allowed to live—as, indeed, I was not fit to live—on the same economical lines as before my illness. I needed more now, and the Lord did provide.

CHAPTER SEVEN

Mighty to Save

RETURNING TO LONDON when sufficiently recovered to resume my studies, the busy life of hospital and lecture-hall was resumed; often relieved by happy Sundays of fellowship with Christian friends, especially in London or Tottenham. Opportunities for service are to be found in every sphere, and mine was no exception. I shall only mention one case now that gave me great encouragement in seeking conversion even when it seemed apparently hopeless.

God had given me the joy of winning souls before, but not in surroundings of such special difficulty. With God all things are possible, and no conversion ever takes place save by the almighty power of the Holy Ghost. The great need therefore of every Christian worker is to know God. Indeed, this is the purpose for which He has given us eternal life, as our Saviour Himself says, in the oft misquoted verse, John 17:3: "This is [the object of] life eternal [not to know but] that they *might* know thee the only true God, and Jesus Christ, whom thou hast sent." I was now to prove the willingness of God to answer prayer for spiritual blessing under most unpromising circumstances and thus to gain an increased acquaintance with the prayer-answering God as One "mighty to save."

A short time before leaving for China it became my duty daily to dress the foot of a patient suffering from senile gangrene. The disease commenced, as usual, insidiously, and the patient had little idea that he was a doomed man, and probably had not long to live. I was not the first to attend to him, but when the case was transferred to me, I naturally became very anxious about his soul. The family with whom he lived were Christians and from them I learned that he was an avowed atheist, and very antagonistic to anything religious. They had, without asking his consent, invited a Scripture reader to visit him, but in great passion he had ordered him from the room. The vicar of the district had also called, hoping to help him; but he had spit in his face, and refused to allow him to speak to him. His passionate temper was described to me as very violent, and altogether the case seemed to be as hopeless as could well be imagined.

Upon first beginning to attend him I prayed much about it; but for two or three days said nothing to him of a religious nature. By special care in dressing his diseased limb I was able considerably to lessen his sufferings, and he soon began to manifest grateful appreciation of my services. One day, with a trembling heart, I took advantage of his warm acknowledgments to tell him what was the spring of my action, and to speak of his own solemn position and need of

God's mercy through Christ. It was evidently only by a powerful effort of self-restraint that he kept his lips closed. He turned over in bed with his back to me, and uttered no word.

I could not get the poor man out of my mind, and very often through each day I pleaded with God, by His Spirit, to save him ere He took him hence. After dressing the wound and relieving his pain, I never failed to say a few words to him, which I hoped the Lord would bless. He always turned his back to me, looking annoyed, but never spoke a word in reply.

After continuing this for some time my heart sank. It seemed to me that I was not only doing no good, but perhaps really hardening him and increasing his guilt. One day, after dressing his limb and washing my hands, instead of returning to the bedside to speak to him, I went to the door, and stood hesitating for a few moments with the thought in my mind, "Ephraim is joined to his idols; let him alone." I looked at the man and saw his surprise, as it was the first time since speaking to him that I had attempted to leave without going up to his bedside to say a few words for my Master. I could bear it no longer. Bursting into tears, I crossed the room and said, "My friend, whether you will hear or whether you will forbear, I must deliver my soul," and went on to speak very earnestly to him, telling him with many tears how much I wished that he would let me pray with him. To my unspeakable joy he did not turn away, but replied, "If it will be a relief to you, do." I need scarcely say that I fell on my knees and poured out my whole soul to God on his behalf. I believe the Lord then and there wrought a change in his soul.

He was never afterward unwilling to be spoken to and prayed with, and within a few days he definitely accepted Christ as his Saviour. Oh, the joy it was to me to see that dear man rejoicing in hope of the glory of God! He told me that for forty years he had never darkened the door of church or chapel, and that then—forty years ago— he had only entered a place of worship to be married, and could not be persuaded to go inside when his wife was buried. Now, thank God, his sin-stained soul, I had every reason to believe, was washed, was sanctified, was justified, in the name of the Lord Jesus Christ and in the Spirit of our God. Oftentimes, when in my early work in China circumstances rendered me almost hopeless of success, I have thought of this man's conversion, and have been encouraged to persevere in speaking the Word, whether men would hear or whether they would forbear.

The now happy sufferer lived for some time after this change, and was never tired of bearing testimony to the grace of God. Though his condition was most distressing, the alteration in his character and behavior made the previous painful duty of attending him one of real pleasure. I have often thought since, in connection with this case and the work of God generally, of the words, "He that goeth forth weeping, bearing precious seed, shall doubtless come again rejoicing, bringing his sheaves with him." Perhaps if there were more of that intense distress for souls that leads to tears, we should more frequently see the results we desire. Sometimes it may be that while we are complaining of the hardness of the hearts of those we are seeking to benefit, the hardness of our own hearts, and our own feeble apprehension of the solemn reality of eternal things, may be the true cause of our want of success.

CHAPTER EIGHT

Voyage to China

SOON AFTER THIS the time so long looked forward to arrived—the time that I was to leave England for China. After being set apart with many prayers for the ministry of God's Word among the heathen Chinese, I left London for Liverpool; and on September 19, 1853, a little service was held in the stern cabin of the *"Dumfries,"* which had been secured for me by the Committee of the Chinese Evangelization Society, under whose auspices I was going to China.

My beloved, now sainted, mother, had come to see me off from Liverpool. Never shall I forget that day, nor how she went with me into the little cabin that was to be my home for nearly six long months. With a mother's loving hand she smoothed the little bed. She sat by my side, and joined me in the last hymn that we should sing together before the long parting. We knelt down, and she prayed—the last mother's prayer I was to hear before starting for China. Then notice was given that we must separate, and we had to say good-by, never expecting to meet on earth again.

For my sake she restrained her feelings as much

as possible. We parted; and she went on shore, giving me her blessing; I stood alone on deck, and she followed the ship as we moved toward the dock gates. As we passed through the gates, and the separation really began, I shall never forget the cry of anguish wrung from that mother's heart. It went through me like a knife. I never knew so fully, until then, what "God so loved the world" meant. And I am quite sure that my precious mother learned more of the love of God to the perishing in that hour than in all her life before.

Oh, how it must grieve the heart of God when He sees His children indifferent to the needs of that wide world for which His beloved, His only begotten Son, died!

> Hearken, O daughter, and consider, and incline thine ear;
> Forget also thine own people, and thy father's house;
> So shall the King desire thy beauty:
> For He is thy Lord; and worship thou Him.

Praise God, the number is increasing who are finding out the exceeding joys, the wondrous revelations of His mercies, vouchsafed to those who "follow him," and emptying themselves, leave all in obedience to His great commission.

It was on September 19, 1853, that the "Dumfries" sailed for China; and not until March 1, in the spring of the following year, did I arrive in Shanghai.

Our voyage had a rough beginning, but many had promised to remember us in constant prayer.

No small comfort was this; for we had scarcely left the Mersey when a violent equinoctial gale caught us, and for twelve days we were beating backwards and forwards in the Irish Channel, unable to get out to sea. The gale steadily increased, and after almost a week we lay to for a time; but drifting on a lee coast, we were compelled again to make sail, and endeavored to beat off to windward. The utmost efforts of the captain and crew, however, were unavailing; and Sunday night, September 25, found us drifting into Carnarvon Bay, each tack becoming shorter, until at last we were within a stone's throw of the rocks. About this time, as the ship, which had refused to stay, was put round in the other direction, the Christian captain said to me, "We cannot live half an hour now: what of your call to labor for the Lord in China?" I had previously passed through a time of much conflict, but that was over, and it was a great joy to feel and to tell him that I would not for any consideration be in any other position; that I strongly expected to reach China; but that, if otherwise, at any rate the Master would say it was well that I was found seeking to obey His command.

Within a few minutes after wearing ship the captain walked up to the compass, and said to me, "The wind has freed two points; we shall be able to beat out of the bay." And so we did. The bowsprit was sprung and the vessel seriously strained; but in a few days we got out to sea, and the necessary repairs were so thoroughly effected on board that our journey to China was in due time satisfactorily accomplished.

One thing was a great trouble to me that night. I was a very young believer, and had not sufficient faith in God to see Him in and through the use of means. I had felt it a duty to comply with the earnest wish of my beloved and honored mother, and for her sake to procure a swimming belt. But in my own soul I felt as if I could not simply trust in God while I had this swimming belt; and my heart had no rest until on that night, after all hope of being saved was gone, I had given it away. Then I had perfect peace; and, strange to say, put several light things together, likely to float at the time we struck, without any thought of inconsistency or scruple. Ever since, I have seen clearly the mistake I made—a mistake that is very common in these days, when erroneous teaching on faith healing does much harm, misleading some as to the purposes of God, shaking the faith of others, and distressing the minds of many. The use of means ought not to lessen our faith in God; and our faith in God ought not to hinder our using whatever means He has given us for the accomplishment of His own purposes.

For years after this I always took a swimming belt with me, and never had any trouble about it; for after the storm was over, the question was settled for me, through the prayerful study of the Scriptures. God gave me then to see my mistake, probably to deliver me from a great deal of trouble on similar questions now so constantly raised. When in medical or surgical charge of any case, I have never thought of neglecting to ask God's guidance and blessing in the use of appropriate means, nor yet of omitting to give Him thanks for answered prayer and restored health. But to me it would appear as presumptuous and wrong to neglect the use of those measures which He Himself has put within our reach, as to neglect to take daily food, and suppose that life and health might be maintained by prayer alone.

The voyage was a very tedious one. We lost a good deal of time on the equator from calms; and when we finally reached the Eastern Archipelago were again detained from the same cause. Usually a breeze would spring up soon after sunset, and last until about dawn. The utmost use was made of it, but during the day we lay still with flapping sails, often drifting back and losing a good deal of the advantage we had gained during the night.

This happened notably on one occasion, when we were in dangerous proximity to the north of New Guinea. Saturday night had brought us to a point some thirty miles off the land; but during the Sunday morning service, which was held on deck, I could not fail to notice that the captain looked troubled, and frequently went over to the side of the ship. When the service was ended, I learned from him the cause—a four-knot current was carrying us rapidly toward some sunken reefs, and we were already so near that it seemed improbable that we should get through the afternoon in safety. After dinner the long-boat was put out, and all hands endeavored, without success, to turn the ship's head from the shore.

After standing together on the deck for some time in silence, the captain said to me, "Well, we have done everything that can be done; we can only await the result." A thought occurred to me, and I replied, "No, there is one thing we have not done yet." "What is it?" he queried. "Four of us on board are Christians," I answered (the Swedish carpenter and our colored steward, with the captain and myself); "let us each retire to his own cabin, and in agreed prayer ask the Lord to give us immediately a breeze. He can as easily send it now as at sunset."

The captain complied with this proposal. I went and spoke to the other two men, and after prayer with the carpenter we all four retired to wait upon God. I had a good but very brief season in prayer, and then felt so satisfied that our request was granted that I could not continue asking, and very soon went up again on deck. The first officer, a godless man, was in charge. I went over and asked him to let down the clews or corners of the mainsail, which had been drawn up in order to lessen the useless flapping of the sail against the rigging. He answered, "What would be the good of that?" I told him we had been asking a wind from God, that it was coming immediately, and we were so near the reef by this time that there was not a minute to lose. With a look of incredulity and contempt, he said with an oath that he would rather see a wind than hear of it! But while he was speaking I watched his eye, and followed it up to the royal (the topmost sail), and there, sure enough, the corner of the sail was beginning to tremble in the coming breeze. "Don't you see the wind is coming? Look at the royal!" I exclaimed. "No, it is only a cat's-paw," he rejoined (a mere puff of wind). "Cat's-paw or not," I cried, "pray let down the mainsail, and let us have the benefit!"

This he was not slow to do. In another minute the heavy tread of the men on the deck brought up the captain from his cabin to see what was the matter; and he saw that the breeze had indeed come. In a few minutes we were plowing our way at six or seven knots an hour through the water. We were soon out of danger; and though the wind was sometimes unsteady, we did not altogether lose it until after passing the Pelew Islands.

Thus God encouraged me, ere landing on China's shores, to bring every variety of need to Him in prayer, and to expect that He would honor the name of the Lord Jesus, and give the help which each emergency required.

CHAPTER NINE

Early Missionary Experiences

O N LANDING IN SHANGHAI on March 1, 1854, I
found myself surrounded with difficulties
that were wholly unexpected. A band of rebels,
known as the "Red Turbans," had taken possession of the native city, against which was en-
camped an Imperial army of from forty to fifty
thousand men, who were a much greater source
of discomfort and danger to the little European
community than were the rebels themselves.
Upon landing, I was told that to live outside the
Settlement[1] was impossible, while within the foreign concession apartments were scarcely obtainable at any price. The dollar, now worth about
three shillings, had risen to a value of eight and
ninepence, and the prospect for one with only a
small income of English money was dark indeed.
However, I had three letters of introduction, and
counted on counsel and help, especially from one
of those to whom I had been commended, whose
friends I well knew and highly valued. Of course
I sought him out at once, but only to learn that

[1] The International Settlement under European control was
established in Shanghai in 1843. It reverted to Chinese hands
by treaty in 1943.

he had been buried a month or two before, having died from fever during the time of my voyage.

Saddened by these tidings, I inquired for a missionary to whom another of my letters of introduction was addressed; but a further disappointment awaited me—he had left for America. The third letter remained; but as it had been given by a comparative stranger, I had expected less from it than from the other two. It proved, however, to be God's channel of help. The Rev. Dr. Medhurst, of the London Mission,[2] to whom it was addressed, introduced me to Dr. Lockhart, who kindly allowed me to live with him for six months. Dr. Medhurst procured my first Chinese teacher; and he, Dr. Edkins, and the late Mr. Alexander Wylie gave me considerable help with the language.

Those were indeed troublous times, and times of danger. Coming out of the city one day with Mr. Wylie, he entered into conversation with two coolies, while we waited a little while at the East Gate for a companion who was behind us. Before our companion came up an attack upon the city from the batteries on the opposite side of the river commenced, which caused us to hurry away to a place of less danger, the whiz of the balls being unpleasantly near. The coolies, unfortunately, stayed too long, and were wounded. On reaching the Settlement we stopped a few minutes to make a purchase, and then proceeded at once to the London Mission compound, where, at the door of the hospital, we found the two poor coolies with whom Mr. Wylie had con-

[2] Usually known as the London Missionary Society.

versed, their four ankles terribly shattered by a cannon ball. The poor fellows declined amputation, and both died. We felt how narrow had been our escape.

At another time, early in the morning, I had joined one of the missionaries on his veranda to watch the battle proceeding, at a distance of perhaps three-quarters of a mile, when suddenly a spent ball passed between us and buried itself in the veranda wall. Another day my friend Mr. Wylie left a book on the table after luncheon, and returning for it about five minutes later found the arm of the chair on which he had been sitting shot clean away. But in the midst of these and many other dangers God protected us.

After six months' stay with Dr. Lockhart, I rented a native house outside the Settlement, and began a little missionary work among my Chinese neighbors, which for a few months continued practicable. When the French joined the Imperialists in attacking the city, the position of my house became so dangerous that during the last few weeks, in consequence of nightly recurring skirmishes, I gave up attempting to sleep except in the daytime. One night a fire appeared very near, and I climbed up to a little observatory I had arranged on the roof of the house to see whether it was necessary to attempt escape. While there a ball struck the ridge of the roof on the opposite side of the quadrangle, showering pieces of broken tile all around me, while the ball itself rolled down into the court below. It weighed four or five pounds; and had it come a few inches higher, would probably have spent its force on me instead of on the building. My dear mother kept the ball for many years. Shortly after this I had to abandon the house and return to the Foreign Settlement—a step that was taken none too soon, for before the last of my belongings were removed the house was burned to the ground.

Of the trials of this early period it is scarcely possible to convey any adequate idea. To one of a sensitive nature, the horrors, atrocities, and misery connected with war were a terrible ordeal. The embarrassment also of the times was considerable. With an income of only eighty pounds a year, I was compelled, upon moving into the Settlement, to give one hundred and twenty for rent, and sublet half the house; and though the Committee of the Chinese Evangelization Society increased my income when, after the arrival of Dr. Parker, they learned more of our circumstances, many painful experiences had necessarily been passed through. Few can realize how distressing to so young and untried a worker these difficulties seemed, or the intense loneliness of the position of a pioneer who could not even hint at many of his circumstances, as to do so would have been a tacit appeal for help.

The great enemy is always ready with his oft-repeated suggestion, "All these things are against me." But, oh, how false the word! The cold, and even the hunger, the watchings and sleeplessness of nights of danger, and the feeling at times of utter isolation and helplessness, were well and wisely chosen, and tenderly and lovingly meted out. What circumstances could have rendered the Word of God sweeter, and the presence of

God so real, the help of God so precious? They were times, indeed, of emptying and humbling, but were experiences that made not ashamed, and that strengthened purpose to go forward as God might direct, with His proved promise, "I will not fail thee, nor forsake thee." One can see, even now, that "as for God, his way is perfect," and yet can rejoice that the missionary path of today is comparatively a smooth and an easy one.

Journeying inland was contrary to treaty arrangements, and attended with much difficulty, especially for some time after the battle of Muddy Flat, in which an Anglo-American contingent of about three hundred marines and seamen, with a volunteer corps of less than a hundred residents, attacked the Imperial camp, and drove away from thirty to fifty thousand Chinese soldiers, the range of our shot and shell making the native artillery useless. Still, in the autumn of 1854 a journey of perhaps a week's duration was safely accomplished with Dr. Edkins, who of course did the speaking and preaching, while I was able to help in the distribution of books,

CHAPTER TEN

First Evangelistic Efforts

A JOURNEY TAKEN in the spring of 1855 with the Rev. J. S. Burdon of the Church Missionary Society (later the Bishop of Victoria, Hong Kong) was attended with some serious dangers.

In the great mouth of the River Yangtze, distant some thirty miles to the north of Shanghai, lies the group of islands of which Tsungming and Haimen[1] are the largest and most important; and farther up the river, where the estuary narrows away from the sea, is situated the influential city of Tungchow, close to Lang-shan, or the Wolf Mountains, famous as a resort for pilgrim devotees. We spent some time in evangelizing on those islands, and then proceeded to Lang-shan, where we preached and gave books to thousands of the devotees who were attending an idolatrous festival. From thence we went on to Tungchow, and of our painful experiences there the following journal will tell:

[1] The island of Haimen disappeared later in the nineteenth century when alluvial deposits united it with the northern bank of the Yangtze River.

Thursday, April 26, 1855

After breakfast we commended ourselves to the care of our heavenly Father, and sought His blessing before proceeding to this great city. The day was dull and wet. We felt persuaded that Satan would not allow us to assail his kingdom, as we were attempting to do, without raising serious opposition; but we were also fully assured that it was the will of God that we should preach Christ in this city, and distribute the Word of truth among its people. We were sorry that we had but few books left for such an important place: the result, however, proved that this also was providential.

Our native teachers did their best to persuade us not to go into the city; but we determined that, by God's help, nothing should hinder us. We directed them, however, to remain in one of the boats; and if we did not return, to learn whatever they could respecting our fate, and make all possible haste to Shanghai with the information. We also arranged that the other boat should wait for us, even if we could not get back that night, so that we might not be detained for want of a boat in case of returning later. We then put our books into two bags, and with a servant who always accompanied us on these occasions, set off for the city, distant about seven miles. Walking was out of the question, from the state of the roads, so we availed ourselves of wheelbarrows, the only conveyance to be had in these parts. A wheelbarrow is cheaper than a sedan, only requiring one coolie, but it is by no means an agreeable conveyance on rough, dirty roads.

We had not gone far before the servant requested permission to go back, as he was thoroughly frightened by reports concerning the native soldiery. Of course we at once consented, not wishing to involve another in trouble, and determined to carry the books ourselves, and look for physical as well as spiritual strength to Him who had promised to supply all our need.

At this point a respectable man came up, and earnestly warned us against proceeding, saying that if we did we should find to our sorrow what the Tungchow militia were like. We thanked him for his kind counsel, but could not act upon it, as our hearts were fixed. Whether it were to bonds, imprisonment, and death, or whether to distribute our Scriptures and tracts in safety, and return unhurt, we knew not; but we were determined, by the grace of God, not to leave Tungchow any longer without the Gospel, nor its teeming thousands to die in uncared-for ignorance of the Way of life.

After this my wheelbarrow man would proceed no farther, and I had to seek another, who was fortunately not difficult to find. As we went on, the ride in the mud and rain was anything but agreeable, and we could not help feeling the danger of our position, although wavering not for a moment. At intervals we encouraged one another with promises from the Scripture and verses of hymns. That verse:

The perils of the sea, the perils of the land,
Should not dishearten thee: thy Lord is nigh at
    hand.

> But should thy courage fail, when tried and sore
>   oppressed,
> His promise shall avail, and set thy soul at rest,

seemed particularly appropriate to our circumstances, and was very comforting to me.

On our way we passed through one small town of about a thousand inhabitants; and here, in the Mandarin dialect, I preached Jesus to a good number of people. Never was I so happy in speaking of the love of God and the atonement of Jesus Christ. My own soul was richly blessed, and filled with joy and peace; and I was able to speak with unusual freedom and ease. And how rejoiced I was when, afterward, I heard one of our hearers repeating to the newcomers, in his own local dialect, the truths upon which I had been dwelling! Oh, how thankful I felt to hear a Chinese, of his own accord, telling his fellow countrymen that God loved them, that they were sinners, but that Jesus died instead of them, and paid the penalty of their guilt! That one moment repaid me for all the trials we had passed through; and I felt that if the Lord should grant His Holy Spirit to change the heart of that man, we had not come in vain.

We distributed a few Testaments and tracts, for the people were able to read, and we could not leave them without the Gospel. It was well that we did so, for when we reached Tungchow we found we had quite as many left as we had strength to carry.

Nearing the end of our journey, as we approached the western suburb of the city, the prayer of the early Christians, when persecution was commencing, came to my mind: "And now, Lord, behold their threatenings, and grant unto thy servants that with all boldness they may speak thy word." In this petition we most heartily united. Before entering the suburb we laid our plans, so as to act in concert, and told our wheelbarrow men where to await us, that they might not be involved in any trouble on our account. Then looking up to our heavenly Father, we committed ourselves to His keeping, took our books, and set off for the city.

For some distance we walked along the principal street of the suburb leading to the West Gate unmolested, and were amused at the unusual title of *heh-kwei-tsi* (black devils) which was applied to us. We wondered about it at the time, but afterward found that it was our clothes, and not our skin, that gave rise to it. As we passed several of the soldiers, I remarked to Mr. Burdon that these were the men we had heard so much about, and that they seemed willing to receive us quietly enough. Long before we reached the gate, however, a tall powerful man, made tenfold fiercer by partial intoxication, let us know that all the militia were not so peaceably inclined, by seizing Mr. Burdon by the shoulders. My companion endeavored to shake him off. I turned to see what was the matter, and at once we were surrounded by a dozen or more brutal men, who hurried us on to the city at a fearful pace.

My bag began to feel very heavy, and I could not change hands to relieve myself. I was soon in a profuse perspiration, and was scarcely able to keep pace with them. We demanded to be taken before the chief magistrate, but were told that they knew where to take us, and what to do with such persons as we were, with the most insulting epithets. The man who first seized Mr. Burdon soon afterward left him for me, and became my principal tormentor; for I was neither so tall nor so strong as my friend, and was therefore less able to resist him. He all but knocked me down again and again, seized me by the hair, took hold of my collar so as to almost choke me, and grasped my arms and shoulders, making them black and blue. Had this treatment continued much longer, I must have fainted. All but exhausted, how refreshing was the remembrance of a verse quoted by my dear mother in one of my last home letters:

> We speak of the realms of the blest,
> That country so bright and so fair,
> And oft are its glories confessed;
> But what must it be to be there!

To be absent from the body! To be present with the Lord! To be free from sin! And this is the end of the worst that man's malice can ever bring upon us.

As we were walking along Mr. Burdon tried to give away a few books that he was carrying, not knowing whether we might have another opportunity of doing so; but the fearful rage of the soldier, and the way he insisted on manacles being brought, which fortunately were not at hand, convinced us that in our present position we could do no good in attempting book distribution.

There was nothing to be done but quietly to submit, and go along with our captors.

Once or twice a quarrel arose as to how we should be dealt with; the more mild of our conductors saying that we ought to be taken to the magistrate's office, but others wishing to kill us at once without appeal to any authority. Our minds were kept in perfect peace; and when thrown together on one of these occasions, we reminded each other that the apostles rejoiced that they were counted *worthy* to suffer in the cause of Christ. Having succeeded in getting my hand into my pocket, I produced a Chinese card (if the large red paper, bearing one's name, may be so called), and after this was treated with more respect. I demanded it should be given to the chief official of the place, and that we should be led to his office. Before this we had been unable, say what we would, to persuade them that we were foreigners, although we were both in English attire.

Oh, the long weary streets that we were dragged through! I thought they would never end; and seldom have I felt more thankful than when we stopped at a place where we were told a mandarin resided. Quite exhausted, bathed in perspiration, and with my tongue cleaving to the roof of my mouth, I leaned against the wall, and saw that Mr. Burdon was in much the same condition. I requested them to bring us chairs, but they told us to wait; and when I begged them to give us some tea, received only the same answer. Round the doorway a large crowd had gathered; and Mr. Burdon, collecting his remaining strength, preached Christ Jesus to them. Our cards and books had been taken in to the mandarin, but he proved to be one of low rank, and after keeping us waiting for some time he referred us to his superiors in office.

Upon hearing this, and finding that it was their purpose to turn us out again into the crowded streets, we positively refused to move a single step, and insisted on chairs being brought. After some demur this was done; we seated ourselves in them, and were carried off. On the road we felt so glad of the rest which the chairs afforded us, and so thankful at having been able to preach Jesus in spite of Satan's malice, that our joy was depicted on our countenances; and as we passed along we heard some say that we did not look like bad men, while others seemed to pity us. When we arrived at the magistrate's office, I wondered where we were being taken; for though we passed through some great gates that looked like those of the city wall, we were still evidently within the city. A second pair of gates suggested the idea that it was a prison into which we were being carried; but when we came in sight of a large tablet, with the inscription "Ming chi fu mu" (the father and mother of the people), we felt that we had been conveyed to the right place; this being the title assumed by the mandarins.

Our cards were again sent in, and after a short delay we were taken into the presence of Ch'en Ta Lao-ie (the Great Venerable Father Ch'en), who, as it proved, had formerly been Tao-tai of Shanghai, and consequently knew the importance of treating foreigners with courtesy. Coming before him, some of the people fell on their knees and bowed down to the ground, and my conductor motioned me to do the same, but without success. This mandarin who seemed to be the highest authority of Tungchow, and wore an opaque blue button on his cap, came out to meet us, and treated us with every possible token of respect. He took us to an inner apartment, a more private room, but was followed by a large number of writers, runners, and other semiofficials. I related the object of our visit, and begged permission to give him copies of our books and tracts, for which he thanked me. As I handed him a copy of the New Testament with part of the Old (from Genesis to Ruth) and some tracts, I tried to explain a little about them, and also to give him a brief summary of our teachings. . . . He listened very attentively, as of course did all the others present. He then ordered some refreshments to be brought in, which were very welcome, and himself partook of them with us.

After a long stay, we asked permission to see something of the city, and to distribute the books we had brought, before our return. To this he kindly consented. We then mentioned that we had been most disrespectfully treated as we came in, but that we did not attach much importance to the fact, being aware that the soldiers knew no better. Not desiring, however, to have such an experience repeated, we requested him to give orders that we were not to be further molested. This also he promised to do, and with every possible token of respect accompanied us to the door of his official residence, sending several runners to see that we were respectfully treated. We distributed our books well and quickly, and left the city quite in state. It was amusing to us to see the way in which the runners made use of their tails. When the street was blocked by the crowd, they turned them into whips, and laid them about the people's shoulders to right and left!

We had a little trouble in finding our wheelbarrows; but eventually succeeding, we paid off the chair coolies, mounted our humble vehicles, and returned to the river, accompanied for fully half the distance by an attendant from the magistrate's office. Early in the evening we got back to the boats in safety, sincerely thankful to our heavenly Father for His gracious protection and aid.

CHAPTER ELEVEN

With the Rev. William Burns

AFTER THE RETAKING OF SHANGHAI by the Imperialists, in February, 1855, I was enabled to rent a house within the walls of the native city, and gladly availed myself of this opportunity to reside amid the crowded population left to inhabit the ruins that had survived the war. Here I made my headquarters, though often absent on more or less prolonged itinerations.

At the suggestion of the Rev. Dr. Medhurst, the veteran leader of the London Mission, I was led at about this period to adopt the native costume in preference to foreign dress, to facilitate travel and residence inland. The Chinese had permitted a foreign firm to build a silk factory some distance inland, with the proviso that the style of building must be purely Chinese, and that there should be nothing external to suggest that it was foreign. Much benefit was found to result from this change of costume, and I, and most of those associated with me, have continued to use native dress.[1]

The Taiping rebellion, commenced in 1851, had by this time reached the height of its

[1] This statement has remained true ever since, though in recent years changing conditions have modified the practice.

ephemeral success. The great city of Nanking had fallen before the invading host; and there, within two hundred miles of Shanghai, the rebels had established their headquarters, and proceeded to fortify themselves for further conquests. During the summer of 1855 various attempts were made to visit the leaders of the movement, in order to bring to bear some decidedly Christian influence upon them; but so little success was met with, that these efforts were abandoned.

I, among others, had sought to reach Nanking; but finding it impossible to do so, turned my attention again to evangelistic work on the island of Tsungming. After some time I was enabled so far to overcome the prejudice and fears of the people as to rent a little house and settle down in their midst. This was a great joy and encouragement to me; but before many weeks were over complaints were made by the local authorities to the British Consul, who compelled me to retire; though the French Consul had himself secured to the Roman Catholic missionaries a property within three or four miles of the house I had to vacate. Sorely tried and disappointed by this unexpected hindrance, I reluctantly returned to Shanghai, little dreaming of the blessing that God had in store for me there.

A few months previously the Rev. William Burns, of the English Presbyterian Mission, had arrived in that port on his return journey from home; and before proceeding to his former sphere of service in the southern province of Fukien, he had endeavored, like myself, without success, to visit the Taiping rebels at Nanking. Failing in this attempt, he made his headquarters in Shanghai for a season, devoting himself to the evangelism of the surrounding populous regions. Thus in the autumn of the year I was providentially led into association with this beloved and honored servant of God.

We journeyed together, evangelizing cities and towns in southern Kiangsu and north Chekiang, living in our boats, and following the course of the canals and rivers which here spread like a network over the whole face of the rich, fertile country. Mr. Burns at that time was wearing English dress; but saw that while I was younger and in every way less experienced, I had the quiet hearers, while he was followed by the rude boys, and by the curious but careless; that I was invited to the homes of the people, while he received an apology that the crowd that would follow precluded his being invited. After some weeks of observation he also adopted the native dress, and enjoyed the increased facilities which it gave.

Those happy months were an unspeakable joy and privilege to me. His love for the Word was delightful, and his holy, reverential life and constant communings with God made fellowship with him satisfying to the deep cravings of my heart. His accounts of revival work and of persecutions in Canada, and Dublin, and in southern China were most instructive, as well as interesting; for with true spiritual insight he often pointed out God's purposes in trial in a way that made all life assume quite a new aspect and value. His views especially about evangelism as the great work of the Church, and the order of lay evangelists as a lost order that Scripture required to be restored, were seed-thoughts which were to prove fruitful in the subsequent organization of the China Inland Mission.

Externally, however, our path was not always a smooth one; but when permitted to stay for any length of time in town or city, the opportunity was well utilized. We were in the habit of leaving our boats, after prayer for blessing, at about nine o'clock in the morning, with a light bamboo stool in hand. Selecting a suitable station, one would mount the stool and speak for twenty minutes, while the other was pleading for blessing; and then changing places, the voice of the first speaker had a rest. After an hour or two thus occupied, we would move on to another point at some distance from the first, and speak again. Usually about midday we returned to our boats for dinner, fellowship, and prayer, and then resumed our outdoor work until dusk. After tea and further rest, we would go with our native helpers to some teashop, where several hours might be spent in free conversation with the people. Not infrequently before leaving a town we had good reason to believe that much truth had been grasped; and we placed many Scriptures and books in the hands of those interested.

The following letter was written by Mr. Burns to his mother at home in Scotland about this time:

Twenty-five Miles from Shanghai,
January 26, 1856

Taking advantage of a rainy day which confines me to my boat, I pen a few lines, in addition to a letter to Dundee, containing particulars which I need not repeat. It is now forty-one days since I left Shanghai on this last occasion. A young English missionary, Mr. Taylor, of the Chinese Evangelization Society, has been my companion during these weeks—he in his boat, and I in mine—and we have experienced much mercy, and on some occasions considerable assistance in our work.

I must once more tell the story I have had to tell already more than once—how four weeks ago, on December 29, I put on the Chinese dress, which I am now wearing. Mr. Taylor had made this change a few months before, and I found that he was, in consequence, so much less incommoded in preaching, etc., by the crowd, that I concluded it was my duty to follow his example. We were at that time more than double the distance from Shanghai that we are now, and would still have been at as great a distance had we not met at one place with a band of lawless people, who demanded money and threatened to break our boats if their demands were refused. The boatmen were very much alarmed, and insisted on returning to some place nearer home. These people had previously broken in, violently, a part of Mr. Taylor's boat, because their unreasonable demand for books was not complied with.

We have a large, very large field of labor in this region, though it might be difficult in the meantime for one to establish himself in any particular place; the people listen with attention, but we need the power from on High to convince and convert. Is there any spirit of prayer on our behalf among God's people in Kilsyth? or is there any effort to seek this spirit? How great the need is, and how great the arguments and motives for prayer in this case. The harvest here is indeed great, and the laborers are few, and imperfectly fitted without much grace for such a work. And yet grace can make the few and feeble instruments the means of accomplishing great things—things greater than we can even conceive.

The incident referred to in this letter, which led to our return to Shanghai more speedily than we had at first intended, took place on the northern border of Chekiang. We had reached a busy market town known by the name of Wuchen, or Black Town, the inhabitants of which, we had been told, were the wildest and most lawless people in that part of the country. Such indeed we found them to be: the town was a refuge for salt smugglers and other bad characters. The following extracts are taken from my journal, written at the time:

January 8, 1856

Commenced our work in Wuchen this morning by distributing a large number of tracts and some Testaments. The people seemed much surprised, and we could not learn that any foreigner had been here before. We preached twice—once in the temple of the God of War, and afterward in an empty space left by a fire, which had completely destroyed many houses. In the afternoon we preached again to a large and attentive audience on the same site; and in the evening adjourned to a teashop, where we had a good opportunity of speaking until it got noised abroad that we were there, when, too many people coming in, we were obliged to leave. Our native assistants, Tsien and Kuei-hua, were able, however, to remain. Returning to our boats, we spoke to a number of people standing on a bridge, and felt we had abundant reason to be thankful and encouraged by the result of our first day's labor.

January 10

First sent Tsien and Keui-hua to distribute some sheet tracts. After their return we went with them, and in a space cleared by fire we separated, and addressed two audiences. On our return to the boats for lunch, we found people waiting, as usual, and desiring books. Some were distributed to those who were able to read them; and then asking them kindly to excuse us while we took our midday meal, I went into my boat and shut the door.

Hardly was there time to pour out a cup of tea when a battering began, and the roof was at once broken in. I went out at the back, and found four or five men taking the large lumps of frozen earth turned up in a field close by—weighing, I should suppose, from seven to fourteen pounds each—and throwing them at the boat. Remonstrance was of no avail, and it was not long ere a considerable part of the upper structure of the boat was broken to pieces, and a quantity of earth covered the things inside. Finally, Tsien got a boat that was passing to land him at a short distance, and by a few tracts drew away the attention of the men, thus ending the assault.

We now learned that of those who had done the mischief only two were natives of the place, the others being salt smugglers, and that the cause was our not having satisfied their unreasonable demand for books. Most providentially no one was injured; and as soon as quiet was somewhat restored, we all met in Mr. Burns's boat and joined in thanksgiving that we had been preserved from personal harm, praying also for the perpetrators of the mischief, and that it might be overruled for good to us and to those with us. We then took our lunch and went on shore, and but a few steps from the boats addressed a large multitude that soon assembled. We were specially assisted; never were we heard with more attention, and not one voice was found to sympathize with the men who had molested us. In the evening, at the teashops, the same spirit was manifested, and some seemed to hear with joy the glad tidings of salvation through a crucified and risen Saviour.

As we came home we passed a barber's shop still open, and I went in, and while getting my head shaved had an opportunity of speaking to a few people, and afterward pasted a couple of sheet tracts on the wall for the benefit of future customers.

A respectable shopkeeper of the name of Yao, who on the first or second day of our stay at Wuchen had received portions of the New Testament and a tract, came yesterday, when our boat was broken, to beg for some more books. At that time we were all in confusion from the damage done, and from the earth thrown into the boat, and so invited him to come again in a day or two's time, when we would gladly supply him.

This morning he appeared and handed in the following note:

> On a former day I begged Burns and Taylor, the two "Rabbis," to give me good books. It happened at that time those of our town whose hearts were deceived by Satan, not knowing the Son of David, went so far as to dare to "raca" and "moreh" and injure your respected boat. I thank you for promising afterwards to give the books, and beg the following: Complete New Testament, Discourse of a Good Man When Near His Death, Important Christian Doctrines, an Almanac, Principles of Christianity, Way to Make the World Happy—of each one copy. Sung and Tsien, and all teachers I hope are well. Further compliments are unwritten.

This note is interesting, as showing that he had been reading the New Testament attentively, as the italicized words were all taken from it. His use of "raca" and "moreh" for reviling, shows their meaning was not lost upon him.

After supplying this man, we went out with Tsien and Kuei-hua to the east of the town, and spoke in the street for a short time. Upon returning to the boats, I was visited by two Chihli[2] men, who are in the magistrate's office here. I was greatly helped in speaking to them of a crucified Saviour in the Mandarin dialect; and though one of them did not pay much attention, the other did, and made inquiries that showed the interest he was feeling. When they had left, I went on shore and spoke to the people collected

[2] This region corresponds approximately to the modern province of Hopeh in northeast China.

there, to whom Kuei-hua had been preaching. The setting sun afforded a parable, and reminded one of the words of Jesus, "The night cometh, when no man can work"; and as I spoke of the uncertain duration of this life, and of our ignorance as to the time of Christ's return, a degree of deep seriousness prevailed that I had never previously witnessed in China. I engaged in prayer, and the greatest decorum was observed. I then returned to my boat with a Buddhist priest who had been in the audience, and he admitted that Buddhism was a system of deceit that could give no hope in death.

January 12

In the afternoon we addressed the people on shore close to our boats, also in one of the streets of the city, and in a teashop, books being distributed on each occasion. In the evening we went as usual to speak in the teashops, but determined to go to the opposite end of the town, in order to afford those who lived there a better opportunity of meeting with us. It was a long straggling place, nearly two English miles in length. As Mr. Burns and I were accustomed to talk together in Chinese, this conclusion was known to those in the boats.

After we had proceeded a short distance we changed our minds, and went instead to the usual teashop, thinking that persons might have gone there expecting to meet us. But this was not the case; and we did not find such serious hearers as we had done on previous occasions. On this account Mr. Burns proposed leaving earlier than usual, and we did so, telling Tsien and Kuei-hua that they might remain a little longer. Returning to the boats, we gave away a few books; but, singularly enough, were left to go alone, no one accompanying us, as is so generally the case. Instead of being a clear night, as it was when we started, we found that it had become intensely dark. On our way we met the boatman, whose manner seemed very strange, and without giving us any explanation he blew out the candle of our lantern; we relighted the lantern, telling him not to put it out again, when to our surprise he deliberately removed the candle and threw it into the canal. He then walked down along a low wall jutting out to the river's edge, and gazed into the water.

Not knowing what was the matter with him, I ran forward to hold him, fearful lest he were going to drown himself; but to my great relief he came quietly back. In answer to our repeated questions he told us not to speak, for some bad men were seeking to destroy the boats, and they had moved away to avoid them. He then led us to the place where one of them was laying. Before long Tsien and Kuei-hua came and got safely on board, and soon after we were joined by the teacher Sung, and the boat moved away.

The cause of all this disturbance was then explained. A man professing to be the constable had come to the boats in our absence, with a written demand for ten dollars and a quantity of opium. He stated that there were more than fifty country people (salt smugglers) awaiting our reply in an adjoining teashop; and if we gave them what they wanted, and three hundred cash to pay for their tea, we might remain in peace; but that if not, they would come at once and destroy our boats. Sung told them that we could not comply with their demand; for, not being engaged in trade, but only in preaching and book distribution, we had not an atom of opium, and that our money was nearly all expended. The man, however, told him plainly that he did not believe him, and Sung had no alternative but to seek us out, desiring the man to await our reply. Not knowing that we had changed our plans, he sought us in the wrong direction, and of course in vain.

In the meanwhile the boatmen had succeeded in moving off. They were very much alarmed; and having so recently had proof of what these men would do in open daylight, felt no desire to experience what they might attempt by night. Moving away, therefore, they had separated, so that if one boat should be injured the other might afford us a refuge. It was after this that we had providentially met the boatman, and had been safely led on board. As Sung repassed the place where we were previously moored, he saw between the trees a dozen or more men, and heard them inquiring where the boats had gone to; but no one could tell. Fortunately they sought in vain.

After awhile the boats joined, and rowed together for some time. It was already late, and to travel by night in that part of the country was not the way to avoid danger from evil men; so the question arose as to what should be done. This we left for the boatmen to decide; they had moved off of their own accord, and we felt that whatever we personally might desire we could not constrain others to remain in a position of danger on our account. We urged them, however, to do quickly whatever they intended to do, as the morrow was the Lord's Day, when we should not wish to travel. We also informed them that wherever we were we must fulfill our mission, and preach the Gospel; it therefore made but little difference where we might stay, for even if we passed the night unperceived, we were sure to be found out on the following morning. The men consequently concluded that we might as well return to the place from which we had started; to this we fully agreed, and they turned back accordingly. But—whether by accident or no we could not tell—they got into another stream, and rowed for some time they knew not whither. At last, as it was very dark, they moored for the night.

We then called the boatmen together, with our native assistants, and read to them Psalm 91. It may be imagined how appropriate to our position and need and how sweetly consoling was this portion of God's Word:

He that dwelleth in the secret place of the most High
Shall abide under the shadow of the Almighty.
I will say of the Lord, He is my refuge and my fortress:
My God; in him will I trust.
Surely he shall deliver thee from the snare of the fowler,
And from the noisome pestilence.

He shall cover thee with his feathers, and under
his wings shalt thou trust:
His truth shall be thy shield and buckler.
Thou shalt not be afraid for the terror by night;
Nor for the arrow that flieth by day.

. . . .

Because he hath set his love upon me, therefore
will I deliver him.
I will set him on high, because he hath known
my name.
He shall call upon me, and I will answer him;
I will be with him in trouble; I will deliver him,
and honor him.
With long life will I satisfy him, and show him
my salvation.

Committing ourselves in prayer to His care and
keeping, who had covered us with thick darkness
and permitted us to escape from the hand of the
violent, we retired for the night; which—thanks
to the kind protection of the Watchman of
Israel, who neither slumbers nor forgets His people—we passed in peace and quietness, and were
enabled, in some measure, to realize the truth of
that precious word, "Thou art my hiding-place,
and my shield."

Sunday, January 13

This morning I was awakened about 4 A.M. by
violent pain in the knee-joint. I had bruised it
the day before, and severe inflammation was the
result. To my great surprise I heard the rain pour-
ing down in torrents, the weather having previously been particularly fine. On looking out,
we found ourselves so near our former stopping
place that, had nothing happened to prevent it,

we should not have felt justified in neglecting to go into the town to preach as usual; but the rain was so heavy all day that no one could leave the boats. Thus we enjoyed a delightful day of rest, such as we had not had for some time; and the weather prevented much inquiry being made for us. Had the day been fine we should most likely have been discovered, even if we had not left the boats. As it was, we were allowed to think in peace, and with wonder and gratitude, of the gracious dealings of our God, who had thus led us apart into "a desert place" to rest awhile.

Monday, January 14

A cloudless morning. One of the native assistants went before daybreak to get some clothes which had been given out for washing. He came back with the tidings that, notwithstanding the drenching rain of yesterday, men had been seeking us in all directions. We had been kept, however, in peace and safety "under the shadow of the Almighty."

The boatmen were now so thoroughly alarmed that they would stay no longer, and moved off at dawn. I was confined to my quarters by lameness, and had no alternative but to go with them. In the afternoon we reached Pingwang, on the way to Shanghai.

> Ill that God blesses is our good,
>   And unblest good is ill;
> And all is right that seems most wrong,
>   If it be His sweet will."

CHAPTER TWELVE

Called to Swatow

HAVING TO LEAVE the neighborhood of Black
Town thus unexpectedly was a real disappointment to us, as we had hoped to spend some
time evangelizing in that district. We were to
prove, however, that no unforeseen mischance
had happened, but that these circumstances
which seemed so trying were necessary links in
the chain of a divinely ordered providence, guid-
ing to other and wider spheres.

God does not permit persecution to arise without sufficient reason. . . . He was leading us by
a way that we knew not; but it was nonetheless
His way.

> O Lord, how happy should we be
> If we would cast our care on Thee,
>   If we from self would rest;
> And feel at heart that One above,
> In perfect wisdom, perfect love,
>   Is working for the best!

When we reached Shanghai, thinking to return inland in a few days with fresh supplies of
books and money, we met a Christian captain
who had been trading at Swatow, and he put very

strongly before us the need of that region, and the fact that there were British merchants living on Double Island, selling opium and engaged in the coolie trade (practically a slave traffic), while there was no British missionary to preach the Gospel. The Spirit of God impressed me with the feeling that this was His call, but for days I felt that I could not obey it. I had never had such a spiritual father as Mr. Burns; I had never known such holy, happy fellowship; and I said to myself that it could not be God's will that we should separate.

In great unrest of soul I went one evening, with Mr. Burns, to take tea at the house of the Rev. R. Lowrie, of the American Presbyterian Mission, at the South Gate of Shanghai. After tea Mrs. Lowrie played over to us "The Missionary Call." I had never heard it before, and it greatly affected me. My heart was almost broken before it was finished, and I said to the Lord, in the words that had been sung—

And I will go!
I may no longer doubt to give up friends, and idol hopes,
And every tie that binds my heart. . . .
Henceforth, then, it matters not, if storm or sunshine be my earthly lot, bitter or sweet my cup;
I only pray, God, make me holy,
And my spirit nerve for the stern hour of strife.

Upon leaving I asked Mr. Burns to come home with me to the little house that was still my headquarters in the native city, and there, with many tears, told him how the Lord had been leading me, and how rebellious I had been and unwilling to leave him for this new sphere of labor. He listened with a strange look of surprise, and of pleasure rather than pain; and answered that he had determined that very night to tell me that he had heard the Lord's call to Swatow, and that his one regret had been the prospect of the severance of our happy fellowship. We went together; and thus we recommenced missionary work in that part of China, which in later years has been so abundantly blessed.

Long before this time the Rev. R. Lechler, of the Basel Missionary Society, had widely itinerated in the neighborhood of Swatow and the surrounding regions. Driven about from place to place, he had done work that was not forgotten, although ultimately he was obliged to retire to Hong Kong. For more than forty years this earnest-hearted servant of God has continued in "labors more abundant"; and quite recently he has left Hong Kong, with his devoted wife, to return again inland, and spend the strength of his remaining years among the people he has so long and truly loved.

Captain Bowers, the Christian friend who had been used of God in bringing the needs of Swatow before Mr. Burns and myself, was overjoyed when he heard of our decision to devote ourselves to the evangelization of that busy, important, and populous mart. Being about to sail himself on his return journey, he gladly offered us free passages on board the "Geelong," in which we left Shanghai early in the month of March, 1856.

A favorable journey of six days brought us to

Double Island, where we found ourselves landed in the midst of a small but very ungodly community of foreigners, engaged in the opium trade and other commercial enterprises. Unwilling to be in any way identified with these fellow countrymen, we were most desirous of obtaining quarters at once within the native city, situated on a promontory of the mainland, five miles farther up, at the mouth of the Han River. Great difficulty was experienced in this attempt to obtain a footing among the people. Indeed, it seemed as though we should fail altogether, and we were helplessly cast upon the Lord in prayer. Our God soon undertook for us. Meeting one day with a Cantonese merchant, a relative of the highest official in the town, Mr. Burns addressed him in the Cantonese dialect; this gentleman was so pleased at being spoken to by a foreigner in his own tongue that he became our friend, and secured us a lodging. We had only one little room, however, and not easily shall I forget the long, hot summer months in that oven-like place, where toward the eaves one could touch the heated tiles with one's hand. More room or better accommodation it was impossible to obtain.

We varied our stay by visits to the surrounding country; but the difficulties and dangers that encountered us here were so great and constant, that our former work in the North began to appear safe and easy in comparison. The hatred and contempt of the Cantonese were very painful, "foreign devil," "foreign dog," or "foreign pig" being the commonest appellations; but all this led us into deeper fellowship than I had ever known before with Him who was "despised and rejected of men."

In our visits to the country we were liable to be seized at any time and held for ransom; and the people commonly declared that the whole district was "without emperor, without ruler, and without law." Certainly, might was right in those days. On one occasion we were visiting a small town, and found that the inhabitants had captured a wealthy man of another clan. A large ransom was demanded for his release, and on his refusing to pay it they had smashed his ankle-bones, one by one, with a club, and thus extorted the promise they desired. There was nothing but God's protection to prevent our being treated in the same way. The towns were all walled, and one such place would contain ten or twenty thousand people of the same clan and surname, who were frequently at war with the people living in the next town. To be kindly received in one place was not uncommonly a source of danger in the next. In circumstances such as these the preserving care of our God was often manifested.

After a time the local mandarin became ill, and the native doctors were unable to relieve him. He had heard from some who had been under my treatment of the benefit derived, and was led to seek our help. God blessed the medicines given, and grateful for relief, he advised our renting a house for a hospital and dispensary. Having his permission, we were able to secure the entire premises, one room of which we had previously occupied. I had left my stock of medicine and surgical instruments under the care of my friend, the late Mr. Wylie, in Shanghai, and went back at once to fetch them.

Mr. Burns came down from a town called Ampow that we had visited together several times, to see me off, and returned again when I had sailed, with two native evangelists sent up from Hong Kong by the Rev. J. Johnson, of the American Baptist Missionary Union. The people were willing to listen to their preaching and to accept their books as a gift, but they would not buy them. One night robbers broke in and carried off everything they had, with the exception of their stock of literature, which was supposed to be valueless. Next morning, very early, they were knocked up by persons wishing to buy books, and the sales continued; so that by breakfast time they had not only cash enough to procure food, but to pay also for the passage of one of the men to Double Island, below Swatow, with a letter to Mr. Burns's agent to supply him with money. Purchasers continued coming during that day and the next, and our friends lacked nothing; but on the third day they could not sell a single book. Then, however, when the cash from their sales was just exhausted, the messenger returned with supplies.

It was early in July, after about four months' residence in Swatow, that I left for Shanghai, intending to return in the course of a few weeks, bringing with me my medical apparatus, for further work in association with the Rev. William Burns. A new and promising field seemed to be opening before us, and it was with much hopeful anticipation that we looked forward to the future of the work. Marked blessing was indeed in store for the city and neighborhood of Swatow; but it was not the purpose of God that either of us should remain to reap the harvest. Mr. Burns while in the interior was taken up and imprisoned by the Chinese authorities soon after I left, and was sent to Canton. And though he returned to Swatow after the war[1] had broken out, he was called away for other service, which prevented his subsequent return; while my journey to Shanghai proved to be the first step in a diverging pathway leading to other spheres.

The Missionary Call

My soul is not at rest.
There comes a strange and secret whisper to my
    spirit
Like a dream of night,
That tells me I am on enchanted ground.

Chorus for first four verses:

    The voice of my departed Lord, Go, teach
        all nations
    Comes on the night air and awakes my ear.

Why live I here?
The vows of God are on me and I may not stop
    to play with shadows
Or pluck earthly flowers,
Till I my work have done and rendered up account.

And I will go.
I may no longer doubt to give up friends
And idol hopes,

[1] Mr. Taylor refers to the second war between Great Britain and China, which began in 1856.

And every tie that binds my heart to thee, my
country.

Henceforth then it matters not
If storm or sunshine be my earthly lot, bitter or
sweet my cup,
I only pray,
God make me holy and my spirit nerve for the
stern hour of strife.

And when one for whom
Satan hath struggled as he hath for me has gained
at last
That blessed shore
Oh how this heart will glow with gratitude and
love.

Chorus for last verse:

Through ages of eternal years my spirit never
shall repent
That toil and suffering once were mine below.

CHAPTER THIRTEEN

Man Proposes, God Disposes

IT IS INTERESTING TO NOTICE the various events which united, in the providence of God, in preventing my return to Swatow, and ultimately led to my settling in Ningpo, and making that the center for the development of future labors.

Upon reaching Shanghai, great was my dismay to find that the premises in which my medicines and instruments had been stored were burned down, and that all the medicines and many of the instruments were entirely destroyed. To me this appeared a great calamity, and I fear I was more disposed with faithless Jacob to say, "All these things are against me," than to recognize that "all things work together for good." I had not then learned to think of God as the One Great Circumstance "in whom we live, and move, and have our being"; and of all lesser, external circumstances, as necessarily the kindest, wisest, best, because either ordered or permitted by Him. Hence my disappointment and trial were very great.

Medicines were expensive in Shanghai, and my means were limited. I therefore set out on an inland journey to Ningpo, hoping to obtain a

97

supply from Dr. William Parker, a member of the same mission as myself. I took with me my few remaining possessions, the principal being my watch, a few surgical instruments, a concertina, books for the study of Chinese, which in those days were very·expensive; but left behind in Shanghai a portion of my money.

The country through which I had to pass was suffering much from drought; it was the height of summer; and the water in the Grand Canal was very low, having been largely drawn upon for the neighboring rice fields, as well as evaporated by the intense heat. I had determined to make the journey as much of a mission tour as possible, and set out well supplied with Christian tracts and books. After fourteen days spent in traveling slowly through the populous country, preaching and distributing books, etc., we reached a large town called Shihmenwan, and here, finding that my supply of literature was exhausted, I determined not to linger over the rest of the journey, but to reach Ningpo as speedily as possible, via the city of Haining.

August 4, 1856

There was no water beyond Shihmenwan, so I paid off my boat, hired coolies to carry my things as far as to Changwan, and ere sunrise we were on the way. I walked on alone, leaving my servant to follow with the men, who made frequent stoppages to rest; and on reaching a city through which we had to pass, I waited for them in a teashop just outside the North Gate. The coolies came on very slowly, and seemed tired when they arrived. I soon found that they were both opium-smokers, so that, although they had only carried a load that one strong man would think nothing of taking three times the distance, they really seemed wearied.

After some rice and tea and an hour's rest—including, I doubt not, a smoke of the opium pipe—they were a little refreshed, and I proposed moving on, that we might get to Changwan before the sun became too powerful. My servant, however, had a friend in the city, and he desired to spend the day there, and to go on next morning. But to this I objected, wishing to reach Haining that night if possible. . . . We therefore set off, entered the North Gate, and had passed through about a third of the city, when the coolies stopped to rest, and said they should be unable to carry the burden on to Changwan. Finally, they agreed to take it to the South Gate, where they were to be paid in proportion to the distance they had carried it; and the servant undertook to call other coolies and come along with them.

I walked on before as in the first instance, and the distance being only about four miles, soon reached Changwan, and waited their arrival, meanwhile engaging coolies for the rest of the journey to Haining. Having waited a long time, I began to wonder at the delay; and at length it became too late to finish the journey to Haining that night. I felt somewhat annoyed; and but that my feet were blistered, and the afternoon very hot, I should have gone back to meet them and urge them on. At last I concluded that my servant must have gone to his friend's, and would not appear until evening. But evening came, and still there was no sign of them.

Feeling very uneasy, I began diligently to inquire whether they had been seen. At last a man responded, "Are you a guest from Shihmenwan?" I answered in the affirmative. "Are you going to Haining?" "That is my destination." "Then your things have gone on before you; for I was sitting in a teashop when a coolie came in, took a cup of tea, and set off for Haining in a great hurry, saying that the bamboo box and bed he carried, just such as you describe yours to have been, were from Shihmenwan, and he had to take them to Haining tonight, where he was to be paid at the rate of ten cash a pound." From this I concluded that my goods were on before me; but it was impossible to follow them at once, for I was too tired to walk, and it was already dark.

Under these circumstances all I could do was to seek a lodging for the night; and no easy task I found it. After raising my heart to God to ask His aid, I walked through to the farther end of the town, where I thought the tidings of a foreigner's being in the place might not have spread, and looked out for an inn. I soon came to one, and went in, hoping that I might pass unquestioned, as it was already dark. Asking the bill of fare, I was told that cold rice—which proved to be more than "rather burned"—and snakes, fried in lamp-oil, were all that could be had. Not wishing any question to be raised as to my nationality, I was compelled to order some, and tried to make a meal, but with little success.

While thus engaged I said to the landlord, "I

suppose I can arrange to spend the night here?" to which he replied in the affirmative; but bringing out his book, he added—

"In these unsettled times we are required by the authorities to keep a record of our lodgers: may I ask your respected family name?"

"My unworthy family name is Tai," I responded.

"And your honorable second name?"

"My humble name is Ia-Koh" (James).

"What an extraordinary name! I never heard it before. How do you write it?"

I told him, and added, "It is a common name in the district from which I come."

"And may I ask whence you come and whither you are going?"

"I am journeying from Shanghai to Ningpo, by way of Hangchow."

"What may be your honorable profession?"

"I heal the sick."

"Oh! you are a physician," the landlord remarked; and to my intense relief closed the book. His wife, however, took up the conversation.

"You are a physician, are you?" said she; "I am glad of that, for I have a daughter afflicted with leprosy. If you will cure her, you shall have your supper and bed for nothing."

I was curious enough to inquire what my supper and bed were to cost, if paid for; and to my amusement found they were worth less than three halfpence of our money!

Being unable to benefit the girl, I declined to prescribe for her, saying that leprosy was a very intractable disease, and that I had no medicines with me.

The mother, however, brought pen and paper, urging, "You can at least write a prescription, which will do no harm, if it does no good."

But this also I declined to do, and requested to be shown my bed. I was conducted to a very miserable room on the ground floor, where, on some boards raised upon two stools, I passed the night, without bed or pillow, save my umbrella and shoe, and without any mosquito netting. Ten or eleven other lodgers were sleeping in the same room, so I could not take anything off, for fear of it being stolen; but I was, I found, by no means too warm as midnight came on.

August 5

As may be supposed, I arose but little rested or refreshed, and felt very far from well. I had to wait a long time ere breakfast was obtainable, and then there was another delay before I could get change for the only dollar I had with me, in consequence of its being chipped in one or two places. More than three hundred cash also were deducted from its price on this account,[1] which was a serious loss to me in my trying position.

I then sought throughout the town for tidings of my servant and coolies, as I thought it possible that they might have arrived later, or have come on in the morning. The town is large, long, and straggling, being nearly two miles from one end to the other, so this occupied some time. I gained no information, however; and, footsore and weary, set out for Haining in the full heat of the

[1] This represents a loss of about 25 per cent.

day. The journey—about eight miles—took me a long time; but a halfway village afforded a resting place and a cup of tea, both of which I gladly availed myself. When about to leave again, a heavy shower of rain came on, and the delay thus occasioned enabled me to speak a little to the people about the truths of the Gospel.

The afternoon was far spent before I approached the northern suburb of Haining, where I commenced inquiries, but could hear no tidings of my servant or things. I was told that outside the East Gate I should be more likely to hear of them, as it was there the sea-junks called. I therefore proceeded thither, and sought for them outside the Little East Gate, but in vain. Very weary, I sat down in a teashop to rest; and while there a number of persons from one of the mandarin's offices came in, and made inquiries as to who I was, where I had come from, etc. On learning the object of my search, one of the men in the teashop said, "A bamboo box and a bed, such as you describe, were carried past here about half an hour ago. The bearer seemed to be going toward either the Great East Gate or the South Gate; you had better go to the hongs[2] there and inquire." I asked him to accompany me in the search, and promised to reward him for his trouble, but he would not. Another man offered to go with me, so we set off together, and both inside and outside the two gates made diligent inquiries, but all in vain. I then engaged a man to make a thorough search, promising him a liberal reward if he should be successful. In the

[2] That is, the business houses.

meantime, I had some dinner, and addressed a large concourse of people who had gathered together.

When he returned, having met with no success, I said to him, "I am now quite exhausted; will you help me to find quarters for the night, and then I will pay you for your trouble?" He was willing to befriend me, and we set off in search of lodgings. At the first place or two the people would not receive me; for though on our first going in they seemed willing to do so, the presence of a man who followed us, and who, I found, was engaged in one of the government offices, seemed to alarm them, and I was refused. We now went to a third place, and being no longer followed by the mandarin's messenger, we were promised quarters; some tea was brought, and I paid the man who had accompanied me for his trouble.

Soon after he was gone some official people came in; they soon went away, but the result of their visit was that I was told I could not be entertained there that night. A young man present blamed them for their heartless behavior, and said, "Never mind, come with me; and if we cannot get better lodgings for you, you shall sleep at our house." I went with him, but we found the people of his house unwilling to receive me. Weary and footsore, so that I could scarcely stand, I had again to seek quarters, and at length got promise of them; but a little crowd collecting about the door, they desired me to go to a teashop and wait there till the people had retired, or they would be unable to accommodate me.

There was no help for it, so I went, accompanied still by the young man, and waited till past midnight. Then we left for the promised resting place; but my conductor could not find it, and he led me about to another part of the city; and finally, between one and two o'clock, he left me to pass the rest of the night as best I could.

I was opposite a temple, but it was closed; so I lay down on the stone steps in front of it, and putting my money under my head for a pillow, should soon have been asleep in spite of the cold had I not perceived a person coming stealthily toward me. As he approached I saw he was one of the beggars so common in China, and had no doubt his intention was to rob me of my money. I did not stir, but watched his movements, and looked to my Father not to leave me in this hour of trial. The man came up, looked at me for some time to assure himself that I was asleep (it was so dark that he could not see my eyes fixed on him), and then began to feel about me gently. I said to him in the quietest tone, but so as to convince him that I was not, nor had been, sleeping, "What do you want?" He made no answer, but went away.

I was very thankful to see him go, and when he was out of sight put as much of my cash as would not go into my pocket safely up my sleeve, and made my pillow of a stone projection of the wall. It was not long ere I began to doze, but I was aroused by the all but noiseless footsteps of two persons approaching; for my nervous system was rendered so sensitive by exhaustion that the slightest noise startled me. Again I sought protection from Him who alone was my stay, and lay still as before, till one of them came up and began to feel under my head for the cash. I spoke again, and they sat down at my feet. I asked them what they were doing; they replied that they, like me, were going to pass the night there. I then requested them to take the opposite side, as there was plenty of room, and leave this side to me; but they would not move from my feet, so I raised myself up and set my back against the wall.

They said, "You had better lie down and sleep; if you do not, you will be unable to walk tomorrow. Do not be afraid; we shall not leave you, and will see that no one hurts you."

"Listen to me," I replied. "I do not want your protection; I need it not; I am not a Chinese; I do not worship your senseless, helpless idols. I worship God; He is my Father; I trust in Him. I know well what you are, and what your intentions are, and shall keep my eye on you, and shall not sleep."

On this, one of them went away, but soon returned with a third companion. I felt very uneasy, but looked to God for help. Once or twice one of them got up to see if I were asleep. I only said, "Do not be mistaken; I am not sleeping." Occasionally my head dropped, and this was a signal for one of them to rise; but I at once roused myself and made some remark. As the night passed slowly on, I felt very weary; and to keep myself awake, as well as to cheer my mind, I sang several hymns, repeated aloud some portions of Scripture, and engaged in prayer in English, to the great annoyance of my companions, who seemed as if they would have given anything to get me to desist. After that they troubled me no more; and shortly before dawn of day they left me, and I got a little sleep.

August 6

I was awakened by the young man who had so misled me on the previous evening. He was very rude, and insisted on my getting up and paying him for his trouble, and even went so far as to try to accomplish by force what he wanted. This aroused me; and in an unguarded moment, with very improper feeling, I seized his arm with such a grasp as he little expected I was capable of, and dared him to lay a finger upon me again or to annoy me further. This quite changed his manner; he let me quietly remain till the guns announced the opening of the gates of the city, and then he begged me to give him some money to buy opium with. It is needless to say this was refused. I gave him the price of two candles that he said he had burned while with me last night, and no more. I learned he was connected with one of the mandarin's offices.

As soon as possible, I bought some rice gruel and tea for breakfast, and then once more made a personal search after my things. Some hours thus spent proving unavailing, I set out on the return journey, and after a long, weary, and painful walk reached Changwan about noon. Here also my inquiries failed to give me any trace of the missing goods; so I had a meal cooked in a teashop, got a thorough wash and bathed my inflamed feet, and after dinner rested and slept till four in the afternoon.

Much refreshed, I then set off to return to the city, at the South Gate of which I had parted with my servant and coolies two days before. On the way I was led to reflect on the goodness of God, and recollected that I had not made it a matter of prayer that I might be provided with lodgings last night. I felt condemned too that I should have been so anxious for my few things, while the many precious souls around me had caused so little emotion. I came as a sinner and pleaded the blood of Jesus, realizing that I was accepted in Him—pardoned, cleansed, sanctified —and, oh, the love of Jesus, how great I felt it to be! I knew something more than I had ever previously known of what it was to be despised and rejected, and to have nowhere to lay one's head; and I felt more than ever I had done before the greatness of that love which induced Him to leave His home in glory and suffer thus for me; nay, to lay down His very life upon the cross. I thought of Him as "despised and rejected of men, a man of sorrows, and acquainted with grief"; I thought of Him at Jacob's well, weary, hungry, and thirsty, yet finding it His meat and drink to do His Father's will; and contrasted this with my littleness of love. I looked to Him for pardon for the past, and for grace and strength to do His will in the future, to tread more closely in His footsteps, and be more than ever wholly His. I prayed for myself, for friends in England, and for my brethren in the work. Sweet tears of mingled joy and sorrow flowed freely, the road was almost forgotten, and before I was aware of it I had reached my destination. Outside the South Gate I took a cup of tea, asked about my lost luggage, and spoke of the love of Jesus. Then I entered the city, and after many vain inquiries left it by the North Gate.

I felt so much refreshed both in mind and body by the communion I had on my walk to the city that I thought myself able to finish the remaining six miles back to Shihmenwan that evening. First I went into another teashop to buy some native cakes, and was making a meal of them when who should come in but one of the identical coolies who had carried my things the first stage. From him I learned that after I left them they had taken my luggage to the South Gate; there my servant went away, saying on his return that I had gone on, that he did not intend to start at once, but would spend the day with his friend, and then rejoin me; they carried the things to his friend's house, and left them there. I got him to go with me to the house, and there learned that the man had spent the day and night with them, and next morning had called other coolies, and set off for Hangchow. This was all I could gather; so, unable to do anything but proceed on my return journey to Shanghai with all expedition, I left the city again. It was now too late to go to Shihmenwan. I looked to my Father as able to supply all my need, and received another token of His ceaseless love and care, being invited to sleep on a hong-boat,[3] now dry in the bed of the river. The

[3] A passenger boat.

night was again very cold and the mosquitoes troublesome. Still, I got a little rest, and at sunrise was up and continued my journey.

August 7

I felt very ill at first, and had a sore throat, but reflected on the wonderful goodness of God in enabling me to bear the heat by day and the cold by night so long. I felt also that quite a load was now taken off my mind. I had committed myself and my affairs to the Lord, and knew that if it was for my good and for His glory my things would be restored; if not, all would be for the best. I hoped that the most trying part of my journey was now drawing to a close, and this helped me, weary and footsore, on the way. When I got to Shihmenwan and had breakfasted, I found I had still 810 cash in hand; and I knew that the hong-boat fare to Kashing was 120 cash, and thence to Shanghai 360, leaving me just 330 cash—or twelvepence and a fraction—for three or four days' provisions. I went at once to the boat office, but to my dismay found that from the dry state of the river, goods had not come down, so that no boat would leave today and perhaps none tomorrow. I inquired if there were no letter-boats for Kashing, and was told that they had already left. The only remaining resource was to ascertain if any private boats were going in which I could get passage. My search, however, was in vain; and I could get no boat to undertake to go all the way to Shanghai, or my difficulty would have been at an end.

Just at this juncture I saw before me, at a turn

in the canal, a letter-boat going in the direction
of Kashing. This, I concluded, must be one of
the Kashing boats that had been unexpectedly
detained, and I set off after it as fast as hope and
the necessities of the case would carry me. For
the time being weariness and sore feet were alike
forgotten. After a chase of about a mile I over-
took it.

"Are you going to Kashing?" I called out.

"No," was the only answer.

"Are you going in that direction?"

"No."

"Will you give me a passage as far as you do
go that way?"

Still "No," and nothing more.

Completely dispirited and exhausted, I sank
down on the grass and fainted away.

As consciousness returned some voices reached
my ear, and I found they were talking about
me. One said, "He speaks pure Shanghai dialect," and from their own speech I knew them to
be Shanghai people. Raising myself, I saw that
they were on a large hong-boat on the other
side of the canal, and after a few words they sent
their small boat to fetch me, and I went on
board the junk. They were very kind, and gave
me some tea; and when I was refreshed and able
to partake of it, some food also. I then took my
shoes and stockings off to ease my feet, and the
boatman kindly provided me with hot water to
bathe them. When they heard my story, and
saw the blisters on my feet, they evidently pitied
me, and hailed every boat that passed to see if
it was going my way. Not finding one, by and

by, after a few hours' sleep, I went ashore with the captain, intending to preach in the temple of Kwan-ti.

Before leaving the junk I told the captain and those on board that I was now unable to help myself; that I had not strength to walk to Kashing, and having been disappointed in getting a passage today, I should no longer have sufficient means to take me there by letter-boat, which was an expensive mode of traveling; that I knew not how the God whom I served would help me, but that I had no doubt He would do so; and that my business now was to serve Him where I was. I also told them that the help which I knew would come ought to be an evidence to them of the truth of the religion which I and the other missionaries at Shanghai preached.

On our way to the town, while engaged in conversation with the captain, we saw a letter-boat coming up. The captain drew my attention to it; but I reminded him that I had no longer the means of paying my passage by it. He hailed it, nevertheless, and found that it was going to a place about nine English miles from Shanghai, whence one of the boatmen would carry the mails overland to the city. He then said, "This gentleman is a foreigner from Shanghai, who has been robbed, and has no longer the means of returning. If you will take him with you as far as you go, and then engage a sedan chair to carry him the rest of the way, he will pay you in Shanghai. You see my boat is lying aground yonder for want of water, and cannot get away. Now, I will stand surety; and if this gentleman does not pay you when you get to Shanghai, I will do so on your return." This unsolicited kindness on the part of a Chinaman, a perfect stranger, will appear the more remarkable to anyone acquainted with the character of the Chinese, who are generally most reluctant to risk their money. Those on the letter-boat agreeing to the terms, I was taken on board as a passenger. Oh, how thankful I felt for this providential interposition, and to be once more on my way to Shanghai!

Letter-boats such as the one on which I was now traveling are of a long narrow build, and very limited as to their inside accommodation. One has to lie down all the time they are in motion, as a slight movement would easily upset them. This was no irksome condition to me, however; on the contrary, I was only too glad to be quiet. They are the quickest boats I have seen in China. Each one is worked by two men, who relieve one another continuously night and day. They row with their feet, and paddle with their hands; or if the wind is quite favorable, row with their feet, and with one hand manage a small sail, while steering with the other.

After a pleasant and speedy journey, I reached Shanghai in safety on August 9, through the help of Him who has said, "I will never leave thee, nor forsake thee"; "Lo, I am with you alway, even unto the end of the world."

CHAPTER FOURTEEN

Providential Guidance

IT NOW SEEMED VERY CLEAR that the lost property—including everything I possessed in China, with the exception of a small sum of money providentially left in Shanghai—had been deliberately stolen by my servant, who had gone off with it to Hangchow. The first question, of course, was how best to act for the good of the man who had been the cause of so much trouble. It would not have been difficult to take steps that would have led to his punishment; though the likelihood of any reparation being made for the loss sustained was very small. But the consideration which weighed most heavily was that the thief was a man for whose salvation I had labored and prayed; and I felt that to prosecute him would not be to emphasize the teaching of the Sermon on the Mount, in which we had read together, "Resist not evil," and other similar precepts. Finally, concluding that his soul was of more value than the £40 worth of things I had lost, I wrote and told him this, urging upon him his need of repentance and faith in the Lord Jesus Christ. The course I took commended itself to my Christian friends in England, one of whom was afterward led to send me a check for £40—the first of many subsequently received from the same kind helper.[1]

Having obtained the little money left in Shanghai, I again set out for Ningpo, to seek assistance from Dr. Parker in replacing the medicines I had previously lost by fire. This being satisfactorily accomplished, I returned once more to Shanghai, en route for Swatow, hoping soon to rejoin my much-loved friend, Mr. Burns, in the work in that important center. God had willed it otherwise, however; and the delay caused by the robbery was just sufficient to prevent me from starting for the South as I had intended.

Over the political horizon storm clouds had long been gathering, precursors of coming war; and early in October of this year (1856) the affair of the Lorcha "Arrow" at Canton led to the definite commencement of hostilities. Very soon China was deeply involved in a second[2] prolonged struggle with foreign powers; and missionary operations, in the South at any rate, had to be largely suspended. Tidings of these events, together with letters from Mr. Burns, arrived just in time to meet me in Shanghai as I was leaving for Swatow; and thus hindered, I could not but realize the hand of God in closing the door I had so much desired to enter.

While in Ningpo, I had made the acquaintance of Mr. John Jones, who, with Dr. Parker, represented the Chinese Evangelization Society

[1] This was Mr. George Müller of Bristol.
[2] The first occasion was the so-called Opium War of 1839-42.

in that city. Hindered from returning to Swatow, I now decided to join these brethren in the Ningpo work, and set out at once upon the journey. On the afternoon of the second day, when already about thirty miles distant from Shanghai, Mr. Jones and I drew near the large and important city of Sungkiang, and I spoke of going ashore to preach the Gospel to the thronging multitudes that lined the banks and crowded the approaches to the city gates.

Among the passengers on board the boat was one intelligent man, who in the course of his travels had been a good deal abroad, and had even visited England, where he went by the name of Peter. As might be expected, he had heard something of the Gospel, but had never experienced its saving power. On the previous evening I had drawn him into earnest converse about his soul's salvation. The man listened with attention, and was even moved to tears, but still no definite result was apparent. I was pleased, therefore, when he asked to be allowed to accompany me, and to hear me preach.

I went into the cabin of the boat to prepare tracts and books for distribution on landing with my Chinese friend, when suddenly I was startled by a splash and a cry from without. I sprang on deck, and took in the situation at a glance. Peter was gone! The other men were all there, on board, looking helplessly at the spot where he had disappeared, but making no effort to save him. A strong wind was carrying the junk rapidly forward in spite of a steady current in the opposite direction, and the low-lying, shrubless shore afforded no landmark to indicate how far we had left the drowning man behind.

I instantly let down the sail and leaped overboard in the hope of finding him. Unsuccessful, I looked around in agonizing suspense, and saw close to me a fishing boat with a peculiar dragnet furnished with hooks, which I knew would bring him up.

"Come!" I cried, as hope revived in my heart. "Come and drag over this spot directly; a man is drowning just here!"

"*Veh bin*" (It is not convenient), was the answer.

"Don't talk of convenience!" cried I in agony; "a man is drowning, I tell you!"

"We are busy fishing," they responded, "and cannot come."

"Never mind your fishing," I said, "I will give you more money than many a day's fishing will bring; only come—come at once!"

"How much money will you give us?"

"We cannot stay to discuss that now! Come, or it will be too late. I will give you five dollars" (then worth about thirty shillings in English money).

"We won't do it for that," replied the men. "Give us twenty dollars, and we will drag."

"I do not possess so much; do come quickly, and I will give you all I have!"

"How much may that be?"

"I don't know exactly, about fourteen dollars."

At last, but even then slowly enough, the boat was paddled over, and the net let down. Less than a minute sufficed to bring up the body of the missing man. The fishermen were clamorous and indignant because their exorbitant demand was delayed while efforts at resuscitation were being made. But all was in vain—life was extinct.

To myself this incident was profoundly sad and full of significance, suggesting a far more mournful reality. Were not those fishermen actually guilty of this poor Chinaman's death, in that they had the means of saving him at hand, if they would but have used them? Assuredly they were guilty. And yet, let us pause ere we pronounce judgment against them, lest a greater than Nathan answer, "Thou art the man." Is it so hardhearted, so wicked a thing to neglect to save the body? Of how much sorer punishment, then, is he worthy who leaves the soul to perish, and Cain-like says, "Am I my brother's keeper?" The Lord Jesus commands, commands me, commands you, into all the world, and preach the Gospel to every creature." Shall we say to Him, "No, it is not convenient"? Shall we tell Him that we are busy fishing and cannot go? That we have purchased five yoke of oxen, or have married, or are engaged in other and more interesting pursuits, and cannot go? Ere long "we must all appear before the judgment seat of Christ; that every one may receive the things done in his body." Let us remember, let us pray for, let us labor for the unevangelized Chinese; or we shall sin against our own souls. Let us consider who it is that has said, "If thou forbear to deliver them that are drawn unto death, and those that are ready to be slain; if thou sayest, Behold, we knew it not; doth not he that pondereth the

heart consider it? and he that keepeth thy soul,
doth not he know it? and shall not he render to
every man according to his works?" (Prov. 24:
11, 12).

> Through midnight gloom from Macedon,
> The cry of myriads as of one;
> The voiceful silence of despair
> Is eloquent in awful prayer:
> The soul's exceeding bitter cry,
> "Come o'er and help us, or we die."
>
> How mournfully it echoes on,
> For half the earth is Macedon;
> These brethren to their brethren call,
> And by the Love which loves them all,
> And by the whole world's Life they cry,
> "O ye that live, behold we die!"
>
> By other sounds the world is won
> Than that which wails from Macedon;
> The roar of gain is round it rolled,
> Or men unto themselves are sold,
> And cannot list the alien cry
> "O hear and help us, lest we die!"
>
> Yet with that cry from Macedon
> The very car of Christ rolls on:
> "I come; who would abide My day,
> In yonder wilds prepare My way;
> My voice is crying in their cry,
> Help ye the dying, lest ye die."
>
> Jesu, for men of Man the Son,
> Yea, Thine the cry from Macedon;
> Oh, by the kingdom and the power
> And glory of Thine advent hour,
> Wake heart and will to hear their cry;
> Help us to help them, lest we die.

CHAPTER FIFTEEN

Settlement in Ningpo

THE AUTUMN OF 1856 was well advanced before I reached Ningpo, one of the most ancient and influential cities on the coast of China. Opened to the residence of foreigners in 1842 by the treaty of Nanking, it had long been the scene of missionary labors. Within its thronging thoroughfares the busy tide of life runs high. Four hundred thousand human beings dwell within or around the five miles circuit of its ancient wall, every one a soul that Jesus loves, for whom He died.

As winter drew on I rented a native house in Wu-gyiao-deo, or Lake Head Street. It was not then a very comfortable residence. I have a very distinct remembrance of tracing my initials on the snow which during the night had collected upon my coverlet in the large barnlike upper room, now subdivided into four or five smaller ones, each of which is comfortably ceiled. The tiling of an unceiled Chinese house may keep off the rain—if it happens to be sound—but it does not afford so good a protection against snow, which will beat up through crannies and crevices, and find its way within. But however unfin-

120

ished may have been its fittings, the little house was well adapted for work among the people: and there I thankfully settled down, finding ample scope for service—morning, noon, and night.

During the latter part of this year my mind was greatly exercised about continued connection with my society, it being frequently in debt. Personally I had always avoided debt, and kept within my salary, though at times only by very careful economy. Now there was no difficulty in doing this, for my income was larger, and the country being in a more peaceful state, things were not so dear. But the society itself was in debt. The quarterly bills which I and others were instructed to draw were often met by borrowed money, and a correspondence commenced which terminated in the following year by my resigning from conscientious motives.

To me it seemed that the teaching of God's Word was unmistakably clear: "Owe no man anything." To borrow money implied, to my mind, a contradiction of Scripture—a confession that God had withheld some good thing, and a determination to get for ourselves what He had not given. Could that which was wrong for one Christian to do be right for an association of Christians? Or could any amount of precedents make a wrong course justifiable? If the Word taught me anything, it taught me to have no connection with debt. I could not think that God was poor, that He was short of resources, or unwilling to supply any want of whatever work was really His. It seemed to me that if there were any lack of funds to carry on work, then to that degree, in that special development, or at that time, it could not be the work of God. To satisfy my conscience I was therefore compelled to resign connection with the society which had hitherto supplied my salary.

It was a great satisfaction to me that my friend and colleague, Mr. Jones, also of the Chinese Evangelization Society, was led to take the same step; and we were both profoundly thankful that the separation took place without the least breach of friendly feeling on either side. Indeed, we had the joy of knowing that the step we took commended itself to several members of the committee, although as a whole the society could not come to our position. Depending upon God alone for supplies, we were enabled to continue a measure of connection with our former supporters, sending home journals, etc., for publication as before, so long as the society continued to exist.

The step we had taken was not a little trying to faith. I was not at all sure what God would have me do, or whether He would so meet my need as to enable me to continue working as before. I had no friends whatever from whom I expected supplies. I did not know what means the Lord might use; but I was willing to give up all my time to the service of evangelization among the heathen, if by any means He would supply the smallest amount on which I could live; and if He were not pleased to do this, I was prepared to undertake whatever work might be necessary to supply myself, giving all the time that could be spared from such a calling to more distinctly missionary efforts. But God blessed and prospered me; and how glad and thankful I felt when the separation was really effected! I could look right up into my Father's face with a satisfied heart, ready, by His grace, to do the next thing as He might teach me, and feeling very sure of His loving care.

And how blessedly He did lead me on and provide for me I can never, never tell. It was like a continuation of some of my earlier home experiences. My faith was not untried; it often, often failed, and I was so sorry and ashamed of the failure to trust such a Father. But, oh, I was learning to know Him! I would not even then have missed the trial. He became so near, so real, so intimate. The occasional difficulty about funds never came from an insufficient supply for personal needs, but in consequence of minister ing to the wants of scores of the hungry and dy-ing ones around us. And trials far more searching in other ways quite eclipsed these difficulties; and being deeper, brought forth in consequence richer fruits. How glad one is now, not only to know, with dear Miss Havergal, that:

> They who trust Him wholly
> Find Him wholly true,

but also that when we fail to trust fully He still remains unchangingly faithful. He is wholly true whether we trust or not. "If we believe not, he abideth faithful; he cannot deny himself." But, oh, how we dishonor our Lord whenever we fail to trust Him, and what peace, blessing, and triumph we lose in thus sinning against the faithful One! May we never again presume in anything to doubt Him!

The year 1857 was a troublous time, and closed with the notorious bombardment of Canton by the British, and the commencement of our second Chinese war. Rumors of trouble were everywhere rife, and in many places the missionaries passed through not a little danger. In Ningpo this was especially the case, and the preserving care of God in answer to prayer was consequently most marked. When the awful news of the bombardment of Canton reached the Cantonese in Ningpo their wrath and indignation knew no bounds, and they immediately set to work to plot the destruction of all the foreigners resident in the city and neighborhood. It was well known that many of the foreigners were in the habit of meeting for worship every Sunday evening at one of the missionary houses, and the plan was to surround the place on a given occasion and make short work of all present, cutting off afterward any who might be absent.

The sanction of the Tao-t'ai, or chief civil magistrate of the city, was easily obtained; and nothing remained to hinder the execution of the plot, of which the foreigners were of course entirely in ignorance. (A similar plot against the Portuguese a few months later was carried out, and between fifty and sixty were massacred in open daylight.) It so happened, however, that one of those acquainted with the conspiracy had a friend engaged in the service of the missionaries; and anxious for his safety, he was led to warn him of the coming danger, and urge his leaving foreign employ. The servant made the matter known to his master, and thus the little community became aware of their peril. Realizing the gravity of the situation, they determined to meet together at the house of one of their number to seek the protection of the most High, and to hide under the shadow of His wings. Nor did they thus meet in vain.

At the very time we were praying the Lord was working. He led an inferior mandarin, the Superintendent of Customs, to call upon the Tao-t'ai, and remonstrate with him upon the folly of permitting such an attempt, which he assured him would rouse the foreigners in other places to come with armed forces to avenge the death of their countrymen and raze the city to the ground. The Tao-t'ai replied that, when the foreigners came for that purpose, he should deny all knowledge of or complicity in the plot, and so direct their vengeance against the Cantonese, who would in their turn be destroyed; "and thus," said he, "we shall get rid of both Cantonese and foreigners by one stroke of policy." The Superintendent of Customs assured him that all such attempts at evasion would be useless; and, finally, the Tao-t'ai sent to the Cantonese, withdrawing his permission, and prohibiting the attack. This took place at the very time when we were asking protection of the Lord, though we did not become acquainted with the facts until some weeks later. Thus again we were led to prove that:

Sufficient is His arm alone,
And our defense is sure.

I cannot attempt to give any historical record of the events of this period, but ere 1857 terminated Mr. Jones and I were cheered by tokens of blessing. It is interesting to recall the circumstances connected with the first profession of faith in Christ, which encouraged us.

On one occasion I was preaching the glad tidings of salvation through the finished work of Christ, when a middle-aged man stood up, and testified before his assembled countrymen to his faith in the power of the Gospel.

"I have long sought for the truth," said he earnestly, "as my fathers did before me; but I have never found it. I have traveled far and near, but without obtaining it. I have found no rest in Confucianism, Buddhism, or Taoism; but I do find rest in what I have heard here tonight. Henceforth I am a believer in Jesus."

This man was one of the leading officers of a sect of reformed Buddhists in Ningpo. A short time after his confession of faith in the Saviour there was a meeting of the sect over which he had formerly presided. I accompanied him to that meeting, and there, to his former co-religionists, he testified of the peace he had obtained in believing. Soon after, one of his former companions was converted and baptized. Both now sleep in Jesus. The first of these two long continued to preach to his countrymen the glad tidings of great joy. A few nights after his conversion he asked how long this Gospel had been known in England. He was told that we had known it for some hundreds of years.

"What!" said he, amazed. "Is it possible that for hundreds of years you have had the knowledge of these glad tidings in your possession, and yet have only now come to preach it to us? My father sought after the truth for more than twenty years, and died without finding it. Oh, why did you not come sooner?"

A whole generation has passed away since that mournful inquiry was made; but how many, alas, might repeat the same question today? More than two hundred millions in the meanwhile have been swept into eternity, without an offer of salvation. How long shall this continue, and the Master's words, "to every creature," remain unheeded?

CHAPTER SIXTEEN

Timely Supplies

NOT INFREQUENTLY our God brings His people into difficulties on purpose that they may come to know Him as they could not otherwise do. Then He reveals Himself as "a very present help in trouble," and makes the heart glad indeed at each fresh revelation of a Father's faithfulness. We who only see so small a part of the sweet issues of trial often feel that we would not for anything have missed them; how much more shall we bless and magnify His name when all the hidden things are brought to light!

In the autumn of 1857, just one year after I came to settle in Ningpo, a little incident occurred that did much to strengthen our faith in the loving-kindness and ever-watchful care of God.

A brother in the Lord, the Rev. John Quarterman, of the American Presbyterian Mission North, was taken with virulent smallpox, and it was my mournful privilege to nurse him through his suffering illness to its fatal close. When all was over, it became necessary to lay aside the garments worn while nursing, for fear of conveying the infection to others. Not having sufficient money in hand to purchase what was needful in order to make this change, prayer was the only resource. The Lord answered it by the unexpected arrival of a long-lost box of clothing from Swatow, that had remained in the care of the Rev. William Burns when I left him for Shanghai, in the early summer of the previous year. The arrival of the things just at this juncture was as appropriate as it was remarkable, and brought a sweet sense of the Father's own providing.

About two months later the following was penned:

November 18, 1857

Many seem to think that I am very poor. This certainly is true enough in one sense, but I thank God it is "as poor, yet making many rich; as having nothing, yet possessing all things." And my God shall supply all my need; to Him be all the glory. I would not, if I could, be otherwise than I am—entirely dependent myself upon the Lord, and used as a channel of help to others.

On Saturday, November 4, our regular home mail arrived. That morning we supplied, as usual, a breakfast to the destitute poor, who came to the number of seventy. Sometimes they do not reach forty, at other times exceeding eighty. They come to us every day, Lord's Day excepted, for then we cannot manage to attend to them and get through all our other duties too. Well, on that Saturday morning we paid all expenses, and provided ourselves for the morrow, after which we had not a single dollar left between us. How the Lord was going to provide for Monday we knew not; but over our mantelpiece hung two scrolls in the Chinese character—Ebenezer, "Hitherto hath the Lord helped us"; and Jehovah-Jireh, "The Lord will provide"—and He kept us from doubting for a moment. That very day the mail came in, a week sooner than was expected, and Mr. Jones received a bill for $214. We thanked God and took courage. The bill was taken to a merchant and although there is usually a delay of several days in getting the change, this time he said, "Send down on Monday." We sent, and though he had not been able to buy all the dollars, he let us have seventy on account; so all was well. Oh, it is sweet to live thus directly dependent upon the Lord, who never fails us!

On Monday the poor had their breakfast as usual, for we had not told them not to come, being assured that it was the Lord's work, and that the Lord would provide. We could not help our eyes filling with tears of gratitude when we saw not only our own needs supplied, but the widow and the orphan, the blind and the lame, the friendless and the destitute, together provided for by the bounty of Him who feeds the ravens. "O magnify the Lord with me and let us exalt his name together. . . . Taste and see that the Lord is good: blessed is the man that trusteth in him. O fear the Lord, ye his saints: for there is no want to them that fear him. The young lions do lack, and suffer hunger: but they that seek the Lord shall not want any good thing"—and if not good, why want it?

But even $200 cannot last forever, and by

New Year's Day supplies were again getting low. At last, on January 6, 1858, only one solitary cash remained—the twentieth part of a penny—in the joint possession of Mr. Jones and myself; but though tried we looked to God once again to manifiest His gracious care. Enough provision was found in the house to supply a meager breakfast; after which, having neither food for the rest of the day, nor money to buy any, we could only betake ourselves to Him who was able to supply all our need with the petition, "Give us this day our daily bread."

After prayer and deliberation we thought that perhaps we ought to dispose of something we possessed in order to meet our immediate requirements. But on looking round we saw nothing that we could well spare, and little that the Chinese would purchase for ready money. Credit to any extent we might have had, could we conscientiously have availed ourselves of it, but this we felt to be unscriptural in itself, as well as inconsistent with the position we were in. We had, indeed, one article—an iron stove—which we knew the Chinese would readily purchase; but we much regretted the necessity of parting with it. At length, however, we set out to the founder's, and after a walk of some distance came to the river, which we had intended to cross by a floating bridge of boats; but here the Lord shut up our path. The bridge had been carried away during the preceding night, and the river was only passable by means of a ferry, the fare for which was two cash each person. As we only possessed one cash, our course clearly was to return and await God's own interposition on our behalf.

Upon reaching home, we found that Mrs. Jones had gone with the children to dine at a friend's house, in accordance with an invitation accepted some days previously. Mr. Jones, though himself included in the invitation, refused now to go and leave me to fast alone. So we set to work and carefully searched the cupboards; and though there was nothing to eat, we found a small packet of cocoa, which, with a little hot water, somewhat revived us. After this we again cried to the Lord in our trouble, and the Lord heard and saved us out of all our distresses. While we were still upon our knees a letter arrived from England containing a remittance.

This timely supply not only met the immediate and urgent need of the day; for in the assured confidence that God, whose we were and whom we served, would not put to shame those whose whole and only trust was in Himself, my marriage had been previously arranged to take place just fourteen days after this date. And this expectation was not disappointed; for "the mountains shall depart, and the hills be removed, but my kindness shall not depart from thee, neither shall the covenant of my peace be removed." And although during subsequent years our faith was often exercised, and sometimes severely, He ever proved faithful to His promise, and never suffered us to lack any good thing.

Never, perhaps, was there a union that more fully realized the blessed truth, "Whoso findeth a wife findeth a good thing, and obtaineth favor of the Lord." My dear wife was not only a precious gift to me; God blessed her to many others during the twelve eventful years through which she was spared to those that loved her and to China.

Hers had been a life-connection with missionary work in that great empire; for her father, the loved and devoted Samuel Dyer, was among the very earliest representatives of the London Mission in the East. He reached the Straits[1] as early as 1827, and for sixteen years labored assiduously among the Chinese in Penang and Singapore, completing at the same time a valuable font of Chinese metallic type, the first of the kind that had then been attempted. Dying in 1843, Mr. Dyer was never privileged to realize his hopes of ultimately being able to settle on Chinese soil; but his children lived to see the country opened to the Gospel, and to take their share in the great work that had been so dear to his heart. At the time of her marriage, my dear wife had been already living for several years in Ningpo, with her friend, Miss Aldersey, in whose varied missionary operations she was well qualified to render valuable assistance.

[1] That is, the Straits Settlements on the southwestern shore of the Malay Peninsula.

CHAPTER SEVENTEEN

God a Refuge for Us

A SOMEWHAT DIFFERENT though not less manifest answer to prayer was vouchsafed early in 1859. My dear wife was brought very low by illness, and at last all hope of recovery seemed gone. Every remedy tried had proved unavailing; and Dr. Parker, who was in attendance, had nothing more to suggest. Life was ebbing fast away. The only ground of hope was that God might yet see fit to raise her up, in answer to believing but submissive prayer.

The afternoon for the usual prayer meeting among the missionaries had arrived, and I sent in a request for prayer, which was most warmly responded to. Just at this time a remedy that had not yet been tried was suggested to my mind, and I felt that I must hasten to consult Dr. Parker as to the propriety of using it. It was a moment of anguish. The hollow temples, sunken eyes, and pinched features denoted the near approach of death; and it seemed more than questionable as to whether life would hold out until my return. It was nearly two miles to Dr. Parker's house, and every moment appeared long. On my way thither, while wrestling mightily

with God in prayer, the precious words were
brought with power to my soul, "Call upon me
in the day of trouble: I will deliver thee, and
thou shalt glorify me." I was at once enabled to
plead them in faith, and the result was deep,
deep, unspeakable peace and joy. All consciousness of distance was gone. Dr. Parker cordially
approved of the use of the means suggested, but
upon arriving at home I saw at a glance that the
desired change had taken place in the absence of
this or any other remedy. The pinched aspect of
the countenance had given place to the calmness
of tranquil slumber, and not one unfavorable
symptom remained to retard recovery.

Spared thus in answer to prayer the loss of my
own loved one, it was with added sympathy and
sorrow that I felt for Dr. Parker, when, in the
autumn of the same year, his own wife was very
suddenly removed. It being necessary for the
doctor to return at once with his motherless
children to Glasgow, temporary arrangements
had to be made for the conduct of the Mission
Hospital in Ningpo, for which he alone had been
responsible. Under these circumstances he requested me to take up the work, at least so far
as the dispensary was concerned. After a few
days of waiting upon the Lord for guidance, I
felt constrained to undertake not only the dispensary work, but that of the hospital; relying
upon the faithfulness of a prayer-hearing God to
furnish the means required for its support.

The funds for the maintenance of the hospital had hitherto been supplied by the proceeds
of the doctor's foreign medical practice; and with

his departure these ceased. But had not God said that whatever we ask in the name of the Lord Jesus shall be done? And are we not told to seek first the kingdom of God, not means to advance it, and that all these things shall be added to us? Such promises were surely sufficient. Eight days before entering upon this responsibility I had not the remotest idea of ever doing so; still less could friends at home have anticipated it. But the Lord had foreseen the need, and already funds were on the way to supply it.

At times there were not less than fifty inpatients in the hospital, besides a large number who daily attended the outpatient department. Thirty beds were ordinarily allotted to free patients and their attendants; and about as many to opium-smokers, who paid for their board while being cured of the habit. As all the wants of the sick in the wards were supplied gratuitously, in addition to the remedial appliances needed for the outpatient work, the daily expenses were considerable; besides which, a number of native attendants were required, involving their support.

When Dr. Parker handed the hospital over to me he was able to leave money that would meet the salaries and working expenses of the current month, and little more. Being unable to guarantee their support, his native staff retired; and then I mentioned the circumstances to the members of our little church, some of whom volunteered to help me, depending, like myself, upon the Lord; and they with me continued to wait upon God that in some way or other He would provide for His own work. Day by day the stores diminished, and they were all but exhausted when one day a remarkable letter reached me from a friend in England which contained a check for £ 50. The letter stated that the sender had recently lost his father, and had inherited his property; that not desiring to increase his personal expenditure, he wished to hold the money which had now been left to him to further the Lord's work. He enclosed £ 50, saying that I might know of some special need for it; but leaving me free to use it for my own support, or in any way that the Lord might lead me; only asking to know how it was applied, and whether there was need for more.

After a little season of thanksgiving with my dear wife, I called my native helpers into our little chapel, and translated to them the letter. I need not say how rejoiced they were, and that we together praised God. They returned to their work in the hospital with overflowing hearts, and told the patients what a God was ours; appealing to them whether their idols had ever helped them so. Both helpers and patients were blessed spiritually through this remarkable provision, and from that time the Lord provided all that was necessary for carrying on the institution, in addition to what was needed for the maintenance of my own family, and for sustaining other branches of missionary work under my care. When, nine months later, I was obliged through failure of health, to relinquish this charge, I was able to leave more funds in hand for the support of the hospital than at the time I undertook it.

But not only were pecuniary supplies vouchsafed in answer to prayer—many lives were spared; persons apparently in hopeless stages of disease were restored, and success was given in cases of serious and dangerous operations. In the case of one poor man, whose legs were amputated under very unfavorable circumstances, healthy action took place with such rapidity that both wounds were healed in less than two weeks. And more permanent benefits than these were conferred. Many were convinced of the truth of Christianity; not a few sought the Lord in faith and prayer, and experienced the power of the Great Physician to cure the sin-sick soul. During the nine months above alluded to sixteen patients from the hospital were baptized, and more than thirty others became candidates for admission into one or other of the Christian churches in the city.

Thus the year 1860 began with openings on all hands, but time and strength were sadly too limited to admit of their being used to the best advantage. For some time the help of additional workers had been a much-felt need; and in January very definite prayer was made to the Lord of the harvest that He would thrust forth more laborers into this special portion of the great world-field. Writing to relatives at home in England, under the date of January 16, 1860, I thus expressed the deep longing of our hearts:

"Do you know any earnest, devoted young men desirous of serving God in China, who—not wishing for more than their actual support— would be willing to come out and labor here?

Oh, for four or five such helpers! They would probably begin to preach in Chinese in six months time; and in answer to prayer the necessary means for their support would be found."

But no one came to help us then; and under the incessant physical and mental strain involved in the care of the hospital during Dr. Parker's absence, as well as the continued discharge of my other missionary duties, my own health began rapidly to fail, and it became a serious question as to whether it would not be needful to return to England for a time.

It was hard to face this possibility. The growing church and work seemed to need our presence, and it was no small trial to part from those whom we had learned so truly to love in the Lord. Thirty or forty native Christians had been gathered into the recently organized church; and the well-filled meetings, and the warmhearted earnestness of the converts, all bespoke a future of much promise. At last, however, completely prostrated by repeated attacks of illness, the only hope of restoration seemed to lie in a voyage to England and a brief stay in its more bracing climate; and this necessity, painful though it seemed at the time, proved to be only another opportunity for the manifestation of the faithfulness and loving care of Him "who worketh all things after the counsel of his own will."

As heretofore, the Lord was present with His aid. The means for our journey were supplied, and that so liberally that we were able to bring with us a native Christian to assist in translation or other literary work, and to instruct in the language such helpers as the Lord might raise up for the extension of the Mission. That He would give us fellow laborers we had no doubt; for we had been enabled to seek them from Him in earnest and believing prayer for many months previously.

The day before leaving China we wrote as follows to our friend, Mr. W. T. Berger, whom we had known in England, and who had ever strengthened our hands in the Lord while in that distant land:

"We are bringing with us a young Chinese brother to assist in literary work, and I hope also in teaching the dialect to those whom the Lord may induce to return with us."

And throughout the voyage our earnest cry to God was that He would overrule our stay at home for good to China, and make it instrumental in raising up at least five helpers to labor in the province of Chekiang.

The way in which it pleased the Lord to answer these earnest and believing prayers, and the "exceeding abundantly" with which He crowned them, we shall now sketch in brief outline.

CHAPTER EIGHTEEN

A New Agency Needed

MY THOUGHTS are not your thoughts, neither are your ways my ways, saith the Lord. For as the heavens are higher than the earth, so are my ways higher than your ways, and my thoughts than your thoughts."[1] How true are these words! When the Lord is bringing in great blessing in the best possible way, how oftentimes our unbelieving hearts are feeling, if not saying, like Jacob of old, "All these things are against me." Or we are filled with fear, as were the disciples when the Lord, walking on the waters, drew near to quiet the troubled sea, and to bring them quickly to their desired haven. And yet mere common sense ought to tell us that He, whose way is perfect, can make no mistake; that He who has promised to "perfect that which concerneth" us, and whose minute care counts the very hairs of our heads, and forms for us our circumstances, must know better than we the way to forward our truest interests and to glorify His own name.

> Blind unbelief is sure to err
> And scan His work in vain;

[1] Isaiah 55:8, 9.

God is His own Interpreter,
And He will make it plain.

To me it seemed a great calamity that failure of health compelled my relinquishing work for God in China, just when it was more fruitful than ever before; and to leave the little band of Christians in Ningpo, needing much care and teaching, was a great sorrow. Nor was the sorrow lessened when, on reaching England, medical testimony assured me that return to China, at least for years to come, was impossible. Little did I then realize that the long separation from China was a necessary step toward the formation of a work which God would bless as He has blessed the China Inland Mission. While in the field, the pressure of claims immediately around me was so great that I could not think much of the still greater needs of the regions farther inland! And, if they were thought of, could do nothing for them. But while detained for some years in England, daily viewing the whole country on the large map on the wall of my study, I was as near to the vast regions of inland China as to the smallest districts in which I had labored personally for God; and prayer was often the only resource by which the burdened heart could gain any relief.

As a long absence from China appeared inevitable, the next question was how best to serve China while in England, and this led to my engaging for several years with the late Rev. F. F. Gough of the C.M.S., in the revision of a version of the New Testament in the colloquial of Ningpo for the British and Foreign Bible Society. In undertaking this work, in my shortsightedness I saw nothing beyond the use that the Book, and the marginal references, would be to the native Christians; but I have often seen since that, without those months of feeding and feasting on the Word of God, I should have been quite unprepared to form, on its present basis, a mission like the *China Inland Mission*.

In the study of that divine Word I learned that, to obtain successful laborers, not elaborate appeals for help, but, first earnest *prayer to God to thrust forth laborers*, and second, the deepening of the spiritual life of the Church, so that *men should be unable to stay at home*, were what was needed. I saw that the apostolic plan was not to raise ways and means, but *to go and do the work*, trusting in His sure Word who has said, "Seek ye first the kingdom of God and his righteousness, and all these things shall be added unto you."

In the meantime the prayer for workers for Chekiang was being answered. The first, Mr. Meadows, sailed for China with his young wife in January, 1862, through the kind cooperation and aid of our friend Mr. Berger. The second left England in 1864, having her passage provided by the Foreign Evangelization Society. The third and fourth reached Ningpo on July 24, 1865. A fifth soon followed them, reaching Ningpo in September, 1865. Thus the prayer for the five workers was fully answered; and we were encouraged to look to God for still greater things.

Months of earnest prayer and not a few abortive efforts had resulted in a deep conviction that a *special* agency was *essential* for the evangelization of inland China. At this time I had not only the daily help of prayer and conference with my beloved friend and fellow worker, the late Rev. F. F. Gough, but also invaluable aid and counsel from Mr. and Mrs. Berger, with whom I and my dear wife (whose judgment and piety were of priceless value at this juncture) spent many days in prayerful deliberation. The grave difficulty of possibly interfering with existing missionary operations at home was foreseen; but it was concluded that, by simple trust in God, a suitable agency might be raised up and sustained without interfering injuriously with any existing work. I had also a growing conviction that God would have me to seek from Him the needed workers, and to go forth with them. But for a long time unbelief hindered my taking the first step.

How inconsistent unbelief always is! I had no doubt that, if I prayed for workers, "*in the name*" of the Lord Jesus Christ, they would be given me. I had no doubt that, in answer to such prayer, the means for our going forth would be provided, and that doors would be opened before us in unreached parts of the Empire. But I had not then learned to trust God for *keeping* power and grace for myself, so no wonder that I could not trust Him to keep others who might be prepared to go with me. I feared that in the midst of the dangers, difficulties, and trials which would necessarily be connected with such a work, some who were comparatively inexperienced

Christians might break down, and bitterly reproach me for having encouraged them to undertake an enterprise for which they were unequal.

Yet, what was I to do? The feeling of blood-guiltiness became more and more intense. Simply because I refused to ask for them, the laborers did not come forward—did not go out to China—and every day tens of thousands were passing away to Christless graves. Perishing China so filled my heart and mind that there was no rest by day, and little sleep by night, till health broke down. At the invitation of my beloved and honored friend, Mr. George Pearse (then of the Stock Exchange), I went to spend a few days with him in Brighton.

On Sunday, June 25, 1865, unable to bear the sight of a congregation of a thousand or more Christian people rejoicing in their own security, while millions were perishing for lack of knowledge, I wandered out on the sands alone, in great spiritual agony; and there the Lord conquered my unbelief, and I surrendered myself to God for this service. I told Him that all the responsibility as to issues and consequences must rest with Him; that as His servant it was mine to obey and to follow Him—His, to direct, to care for, and to guide me and those who might labor with me. Need I say that peace at once flowed into my burdened heart? There and then I asked Him for twenty-four fellow workers, two for each of eleven inland provinces which were without a missionary, and two for Mongolia; and writing the petition on the margin of the Bible I had with me, I returned home with a heart enjoying rest such as it had been a stranger to for months, and with an assurance that the Lord would bless His own work and that I should share in the blessing. I had previously prayed, and asked prayer, that workers might be raised up for the eleven then unoccupied provinces, and thrust forth and provided for, but had not surrendered myself to be their leader.

About this time, with the help of my dear wife, I wrote the little book, China's Spiritual Need and Claims. Every paragraph was steeped in prayer. With the help of Mr. Berger, who had given valued aid in the revision of the manuscript, and who bore the expense of printing an edition of 3,000 copies, they were soon put in circulation. I spoke publicly of the proposed work as opportunity permitted, especially at the Perth and Mildmay Conferences of 1865, and continued in prayer for fellow workers, who were soon raised up, and after due correspondence were then invited to my home, then in the east of London. When one house became insufficient, the occupant of the adjoining house moved, and I was able to rent it; and when that in its turn became insufficient, further accommodation was provided close by. Soon there were a number of men and women under preparatory training, and engaging in evangelistic work which tested in some measure their qualifications as soul-winners.

CHAPTER NINETEEN

The Formation of the C.I.M.

I T WAS THUS that in the year 1865 the China Inland Mission was organized; and the workers already in the field were incorporated into it. Mr. W. T. Berger, then residing at Saint Hill, near East Grinstead, without whose help and encouragement I could not have gone forward, undertook the direction of the home department of the work during my anticipated absence in China; and I proposed, as soon as arrangements could be completed, to go out with the volunteers and take the direction of the work in the field. For the support of the workers already in China, our friends at home were sending in unsolicited contributions from time to time, and every need was met.

We had now, however, to look forward to the outgoing of a party of sixteen or seventeen, and estimated that from £1500 to £2000 might be required to cover outfits, passage money, and initial expenses. I wrote a little pamphlet, calling it *Occasional Paper, No. 1* (intending in successive numbers to give to donors and friends accounts of the work wrought through us in China), and in that paper stated the anticipated needs for floating the enterprise. I expected that God would incline the hearts of some of the readers to send contributions: I had determined never to use personal solicitation, or to make collections, or to issue collecting-books. Missionary boxes were thought unobjectionable, and we had a few prepared for those who might ask for them, and have continued to use them ever since.

It was February 6, 1866, when I sent my manuscript of *Occasional Paper No. 1*, with a design for the cover, to the printer. On the same date a daily prayer meeting, from twelve to one o'clock, had been commenced to ask for the needed funds. And that we did not ask in vain the following figures of amounts will show:

1864 January-December . .	£51	14s. 0d.
1865 January-June	£221	12s. 6d.
June-December . . .	£923	12s. 8d.
1866 January-February 6 . .	£170	8s. 3d.
February 6-March 12 .	£1974	5s. 11d.
March 12-April 18 . .	£529	0s. 0d.[1]

On February 6, 1866, we felt much encouraged by the receipt of £170 8s. 3d. in little more than a month, as it was entirely unsolicited by us—save from God. But it was also evident that we must ask the Lord to do yet greater things for us, or it would be impossible for a party of from ten to sixteen to leave in the middle of May. *Daily united prayer was therefore offered to God* for the funds needful for the outfits and passages of as many as He would have to go out in May.

[1] £ = one pound. s. = shilling.
d. = pence.

Owing to delays in engraving and printing the *Occasional Paper*, it was not ready for the publisher until March 12. On this day I again examined my mission cash-box and the comparison of the result of the two similar periods of one month and six days each, one before and one after special prayer for £1500 to £2000, was very striking.

"This, it will be noticed, was previous to the circulation of the *Occasional Paper*, and, consequently, was not the result of it. It was the response of a faithful God to the united prayers of those whom He had called to serve Him in the Gospel of His dear Son.

"We can now compare with these two periods a third of the same extent. From March 12 to April 18 the receipts were £529, showing that when God had supplied the special need, the special supply also ceased. Truly there is a living God, and He is the hearer and answerer of prayer."

But this gracious answer to prayer made it a little difficult to circulate *Occasional Paper, No. 1*, for it stated as a need that which was already supplied. The difficulty was obviated by the issue with each copy of a colored inset stating that the funds for outfit and passage were already in hand in answer to prayer. We were reminded of the difficulty of Moses—not a very common one in the present day—and of the proclamation he had to send through the camp to the people to prepare no more for the building of the Tabernacle, as the gifts in hand were already too much. We are convinced that if there were less solicitation for money and more dependence upon the power of the Holy Ghost and upon the deepening of spiritual life, the experience of Moses would be a common one in every branch of Christian work.

Preparations for sailing to China were at once proceeded with. About this time I was asked to give a lecture on China in a village not very far from London, and agreed to do so on condition that there should be no collection, and that this should be announced on the bills. The gentleman who invited me, and who kindly presided as chairman, said he had never had that condition imposed before. He accepted it, however, and the bills were issued accordingly for May 2 and 3. With the aid of a large map, something of the extent and population and deep spiritual need of China was presented, and many were evidently impressed.

At the close of the meeting the chairman said that by my request it had been intimated on the bills that there would be no collection; but he felt that many present would be distressed and burdened if they had not the opportunity of contributing something toward the good work proposed. He trusted that as the proposition emanated entirely from himself, and expressed, he felt sure, the feelings of many in the audience, I should not object to it. I begged, however, that the condition agreed to might be carried out; pointing out among other reasons for making no collection, that the very reason adduced by our kind chairman was, to my mind, one of the strongest for not making it. My wish was, not that those present should be relieved by making such contribution as might there and then be convenient, under the influence of a present emotion; but that each one should go home burdened with the deep need of China, and ask of God what He would have them to do. If, after thought and prayer, they were satisfied that a pecuniary contribution was what He wanted of them, it could be given to any missionary society having agents in China; or it might be posted to our London office, but that perhaps in many cases what God wanted was *not* money contribution, but personal consecration to His service abroad; or the giving up of son or daughter—more precious than silver or gold—to His service. I added that I thought the tendency of a collection was to leave the impression that the all-important thing was money, whereas no amount of money could convert a single soul; that what was needed was that men and women filled with the Holy Ghost should give *themselves* to the work: for the support of such there would never be a lack of funds. As my wish was evidently very strong, the chairman kindly yielded to it, and closed the meeting. He told me, however, at the supper table, that he thought it was a mistake on my part, and that, notwithstanding all I had said, a few persons had put some little contributions into his hands.

Next morning at breakfast, my kind host came in a little late, and acknowledged to not having had a very good night. After breakfast he asked me to his study and giving me the contributions handed to him the night before, said, "I thought last night, Mr. Taylor, that you were in the wrong about a collection; I am now convinced you were quite right. As I thought in the night of that stream of souls in China ever passing onward into the dark, I could only cry as you suggested, 'Lord, what wilt Thou have me to do?' I think I have obtained the guidance I sought, and here it is. He handed me a check for £ 500, adding that if there had been a collection he would have given a few pounds to it, but now this check was the result of having spent no small part of the night in prayer.

I need scarcely say how surprised and thankful I was for this gift. I had received at the breakfast table a letter from Messrs. Killick, Martin & Co., shipping agents, in which they stated that they could offer us the whole passenger accommodation of the ship "Lammermuir." I went direct to the ship, found it in every way suitable, and paid the check on account. As above stated, the funds deemed needed had been already in hand for some time; but the coincidence of the simultaneous offer of the ship accommodation and this munificent gift—God's "exceeding abundantly"—greatly encouraged my heart.

On May 26 we sailed for China in the "Lammermuir," a party of sixteen missionaries out of twenty-two passengers. Mr. Berger took charge of the home department, and thus the China Inland Mission was fully inaugurated.

Epilogue

BY DAVID BENTLEY-TAYLOR

WHEN THE "Lammermuir" party arrived in China in 1866 they faced the apparently hopeless task of reaching and evangelizing the interior of the country. But they brought to it the weapons of faith and prayer, and from their base at Hangchow and Ningpo they slowly extended their operations southward into the coastal province of Chekiang. Then, as the new workers gained experience, they moved out into Kiangsu, Anhwei, and Kiangsi. To do this was the work of about ten years, during which they suffered much from sickness and death and the bitter opposition of unruly mobs, who frequently drove them out of cities in which they were attempting to settle and proclaim the Gospel. Beyond them the greater part of inland China was still without Protestant witnesses for Christ, and it was not until 1876 that God, having brought to them substantial reinforcements, fully opened the way into the interior. Then in two remarkable years the pioneers were able to penetrate southwest to the Burma border, northwest to Mongolia and central Asia, and deep into Tibetan lands. When the vast population of China and the geographical size of the country are remembered, this must be recognized as a feat without parallel in the annals of modern missionary endeavor. It was accomplished through persistent prayer and sacrifice not only on the part of those on the field, but also from their friends and supporters at home.

This initial penetration and exploration of the region in which the China Inland Mission was called to preach Christ was followed by a period of consolidation which lasted from 1878 until 1900. During this time the membership of the Mission grew until it numbered within its ranks many hundreds of men and women drawn from the British Isles, North America, Australasia, Scandinavia, Germany, Switzerland, and other lands. These were all united under the general direction of Mr. Hudson Taylor, agreeing to sink minor differences of nationality and denomination in their common loyalty to the Lord Jesus Christ and to the central truths of the Gospel revealed in the Scriptures. Their primary concern was to win souls for Christ and to build them up into a living church worthy of His name. In this pioneer period of the Mission's history visible results were not very large, and the majority of those who turned to Christ were simple country folk of little education. The missionary was unpopular, suspected, and despised by the more educated sections of Chinese society. He was usually the leader of the Christian community in the district where he lived; around him its life revolved and it was chiefly through him that its activities were financed.

In 1900 this infant church and growing Mission were called to pass through the great ordeal of the Boxer rising. In three summer months the C.I.M. alone lost fifty-six missionaries and twenty-three children by martyrdom, while hundreds of Chinese Christians were killed and many other members of the Mission endured extremes of suffering as they tried to reach places of safety. In retrospect this extensive sacrifice of life and health marks a turning point in the story of the work of God in inland China and terminates the strictly pioneer era of the Mission. It was succeeded by a decade when the missionary, frequently regarded as the representative of western civilization, became embarrassingly popular. Multitudes sought association with him from quite unworthy motives, but such a situation also provided unique opportunities and during this time every phase of the work underwent expansion. It was in these days of encouraging response to the Gospel that Hudson Taylor died at Changsha in the heart of inland China, thus crowning a life of Christlike devotion and undaunted witness to which it is difficult to find many parallels. Few missionaries have seen their prayers so vividly answered and their heart's desire so largely fulfilled.

The work he had left was subjected to a further severe test when the Chinese Revolution of 1911 broke up the comparative security of the preceding ten years and ushered in a long period of civil war. Amid desperate conditions of lawlessness, brigandage, and bloodshed the work of building the Church of Christ and proclaiming the Gospel continued with increasing fruitfulness, especially among some of the aboriginal tribes, who turned in large numbers to Christianity. The international fellowship of the Mission survived the strain of the first World War, but conditions in China deteriorated still further after its close. From 1920 onward atheism and further revolution began to be more strenuously advocated, until in the years 1926-7 it became necessary for the third time for most missionaries to be withdrawn to places of safety at the coast. As on previous occasions, however, it was not long before they were back in the interior again, and once more adversity turned out for the furtherance of the Gospel. From 1927 it became a more explicitly avowed principle of the Mission's work that leadership in Christian churches should be transferred from the foreign missionary to Chinese Christians. It is easy now to see that without this transition a strong indigenous church could never have arisen. In course of time foreign funds came to be little used except for the support of foreign workers, while the main initiative in the work and the direction of the churches were undertaken by Chinese believers to whom God had given spiritual gifts. During this period when missionaries stepped into the background of organized church life the C.I.M. called for large reinforcements of men and women to bring the Gospel to the many millions of people who still lived far beyond its sound. As a result two hundred new workers sailed from the homelands during 1929-30 and the Mission's membership rose to its peak of 1,387 in 1936.

Just when it seemed that under the nationalist government an era of greater stability was about to dawn, the conflict with Japan flared up, and before long the China Inland Mission was divided into a minority living in areas occupied by Japanese forces and the remainder in so-called "free China." All the former were interned after the attack on Pearl Harbor at the close of 1941 and they did not regain their freedom until 1945. The Mission's workers in the West were compelled to withdraw before the advancing Japanese, while reinforcements from home were almost entirely cut off so that at one time the active membership of the Mission was reduced to about 250. Yet these years of apparent frustration were rich in blessing. Bible schools for the training of Chinese Christian leaders started to multiply during and immediately after the war. A remarkable work of God in the universities brought hundreds of students to faith in Christ and began to replenish the ranks of Chinese pastors with a new type of leadership. And when the whole land was thrown open again in 1945 it was found that in the main the churches iso lated for so long had grown and prospered.

But it was only after 1945 that the greatest reaping time of all commenced. Missionaries detained at home by the war, or released from internment, poured back into China to take advantage of a rising tide of spiritual opportunity. The tribulations of the past seemed to have plowed up the soul of China, making it ground well prepared for the message of salvation through Jesus Christ. The things for which Hudson Taylor and the early workers had toiled and prayed were now granted on quite a large scale to their successors. Big meetings became a feature of the work in some places and considerable numbers of people from all strata of society were converted. The possibilities of the immediate future seemed boundless, until the tide of civil war surged forward, and in the autumn of 1948 the land began to pass under the control of communists.

This momentous revolution ushered in an entirely new situation. Authorities tolerant or even favorable to missionaries and Christian work were supplanted by those whose whole outlook upon life was based upon atheism, materialism, and hostility to influences emanating from the West. Large meetings became impossible, persecution grew, Christians were suspected of reactionary tendencies, foreigners were severely restricted in their movements, new recruits were unable to sail, and the total number of missionaries in China was rapidly reduced. No man can measure the precise significance of these trends nor foresee what future the Lord may have for the work which He caused Hudson Taylor to bring into being. But it is encouraging to see that all the major setbacks and apparent disasters of the past have proved eventually to be but steppingstones to greater things. Certain it is that this work to which God called His servant in 1865 has been the means whereby a very large number of Chinese have found salvation and hundreds of Christian churches have come into existence where formerly the name of Christ was not known. To God be all the glory. Whatever may be the official attitude to foreign missionaries, the Gospel has taken such deep root in

China that the witness of Chinese Christians will undoubtedly continue.

A life like Hudson Taylor's, leading to such widespread results, deserves close examination, and it has received it at the hands of Dr. and Mrs. Howard Taylor, whose two-volume biography, still in print, is a most moving account both of Hudson Taylor himself and of the fortunes of the Mission up to his death in 1905.

To this *A Retrospect* forms an ideal introduction, and we invite the reader to enjoy the fuller record of these wonderful events and to share by prayer in carrying out the command of the Lord Jesus Christ to preach the Gospel to every creature. The power of prayer cannot be diminished by distance; it is not limited by age, infirmity, or daily duty; political changes and restrictions cannot alter its effectivenes; for the word still stands, "If ye shall ask anything in my name I will do it." The power of prayer in the life of an obedient Christian can only be undermined by neglect.

Over one of the entrances to the China Inland Mission buildings in London stands the text so dear to Hudson Taylor, "Have faith in God." On either side of it, graven in Chinese characters are the two scripture mottos which he first proved true in his early days as a missionary, "Hitherto hath the Lord helped us," and "The Lord will provide." In this spirit we look back and in this confidence we face the future.

MEN OF FAITH SERIES

Eric Liddell
George Müller
Hudson Taylor
Samuel Morris

OTHER BIOGRAPHIES FROM BETHANY HOUSE

Autobiography of Charles Finney (Wessel)
Flight to Heaven (Black)
Jesus (Anderson)
Jesus Freaks: Martyrs (dc Talk)
Jesus Freaks 2: Revolutionaries (dc Talk)
William & Catherine (Yaxley)